DON'T "LOOK OUT!" LOOK IN...

THE POWER IN YOU

ALEXANDRIA GEESON

ISBN: 978-0-9957451-0-0

Dedicated to my mum.
A woman who really has proven that you can change any aspect of yourself for the better

...and my husband Bryan. My number one fan.

CONTENTS

ACKNOWLEDGMENTS

Sincere gratitude and thanks to:

My husband who has always shown such huge faith in me. My biggest fan. Thank you Bryan.

My younger children Ben, William and Sion for putting up with my constant discussions about the book as it progressed. I am sure you are all very relieved that it is finally finished!

My daughter Hannah who was one of the first to read the manuscript. It was a very nerve wracking moment handing it over to you and your husband Sean, but your beautiful comments will never be forgotten.

To my mum who I have joint dedicated this book to. Thank you for your constant encouragement and support.

My sister Krissy. You definitely had the hardest part. Thank you for all your help with advice and editing. The book would not be what it is without all your hard work.

PREFACE

In my lifetime, I have experienced some remarkable things. Some experiences were the most wonderful, whilst others were not. Alongside everyday events, I have experienced immense happiness, and also immense pain. These circumstances alone could be the inspiration for me to write; however, there is something else. I have also been exposed to incidents that I could not have expected to experience. To the point where I could say that they even made me question reality.

As a very young child I had an accident that left me unconscious. Whilst in this unconscious state I had what tends to be called a near death experience. The pain that occurred initially after my fall suddenly went. I was floating down a tunnel of pure light. Happy experiences of my short life were whizzing by me. I felt a deep sense of pure bliss. That feeling is one I will never forget even though I have never felt anything like it since. I became aware of my friend's cries, screaming out my name. I understood that she was scared. I instinctively knew I had a choice. I could choose to carry on down this tunnel or return. As quickly as I made the decision to be back with my friend, I was back, on the floor where I'd collapsed and in pain once more. I was only five years old when this incident occurred and the memories of it still remain.

I felt then, as I still do now, a deep belief that there is more to life than just existing and then death. Is there more to what we perceive and if so could there be more to us than may initially be obvious? I have experienced other strange phenomena, some of which will be discussed in this book. I regularly wonder if perhaps we could be missing the bigger picture, and I am definitely not alone with these wonderings.

Is the full extent of our personal capabilities hidden from our clear view? Abilities that exist, if we just take the time to look deeper? In my personal search, I reached a belief. I couldn't go so far as saying I have reached certain knowledge, since, for something to be truly known, we need to be able to experience it again and again and show the results to others. This sort of 'knowing' seems to be so very important in our world today. But I believe we can have a knowledge that is true to us, even if we cannot fully grasp all of the essential elements. Putting into words a phenomenon is difficult when the words we use in language can't express all that we experience.

My genuine desire for writing this book is a hope that the reader, that is you, will take time to look a little deeper into yourself and the life you see around you. Realise that life does not have to be difficult. We could all be enjoying the riches that life on Earth can bring. We could start living life as an adventure, because, I genuinely believe it is!

INTRODUCTION

It's been said that hell is the moment just before death, when you meet the person you could have become. The *you* who did not hold back. The *you* who made the most of every opportunity available. However, this meeting could only be hell if the *you* that you meet is not the person you actually became. How dreadful would it be to see the *you* that had achieved everything you had always desired? This possibility drives me in attempting to achieve as much in my lifetime as I possibly can. It would be great to end my days on this Earth appreciative of the things I have achieved, happy with the experiences I have experienced and enjoying the memories I have made. I want to be able to face myself, proud of the person I became and elated with the life I lived. No regrets. How about you? Could you start to work on yourself and the life you are living now? Could it possibly be the best investment that you make? Invest in your happiness. Invest in creating worthwhile memories. Invest in your relationships and invest in your personal success. Is there anything that could be more worthwhile?

Nothing you have experienced up to this point should stop you from achieving your dreams in life. Bad starts, bad experiences, bad decisions; none of them should stop you from improving from this point on. These negatives can sometimes be the best teaching tools ever. They can certainly teach us what we don't want in life, which in itself is a valuable lesson. Everyone has had their own fair share of bad luck – some more than others. Negative elements in your life can be changed. It does not matter how old you are, your gender, your social position or your circumstances; there should be nothing that can keep you from improving. Believe it, work on you and anything is possible.

Years back, I was watching a gardening programme where someone had bought a sapling to plant. They had staked the fragile, thin trunk of the tree to stop the winds from bending it, in fear that this would cause the trunk of the tree to break. A professional gardener came along and explained that protecting the tree to this extent would actually stop it from growing strong, as it would never be able to cope with the powerful winds. The professional gardener explained that the tree needed the stake for some support but it also needed the flexibility to be blown about. The force of the wind bending the trunk is how the tree trunk would grow thick and strong, until eventually no stake would be needed. This made me think about life. We all need obstacles in life – they enable us to grow strong. If protected too much, we do not learn to cope with life's struggles. Our past issues can make us stronger and more resilient. So if your life has been full of battles and problems hold your head up high and realise that these conditions have made you a stronger person in the long run. This strength you can now use for your benefit.

You are already capable of living the life you desire. Inside of you lies all of the potential you need to be the happiest and most successful version of yourself. At this point in your life you might not realise how to accomplish your full potential, but the gift is definitely within you. You have the know-how that will enable you to lead the most amazing life. Some of us know the secrets of our Universe, but others do not. We can all learn these secrets – it is never too late. Life does not have to be about struggling and sacrifice; life can be about joy and fulfilment.

Many people are realising that something has been amiss in their life. Perhaps not quite able to put their finger on the exact issue but still knowing, deep inside, that something isn't quite right. Even something as important as what we perceive as our reality is being questioned by some. Could you become happier, more successful and healthier? Could your wildest ambitions become your absolute reality? I believe they can. I am convinced that we can all have a life that fulfils our deepest needs. This may sound fanciful, but I do believe that life has a magical aspect to it which we can all behold if we just choose to look closer and see. The natural world is magical, and we are not exempt from this wonder. At this point you may not realise how to bring about this wonder into your life, but that really doesn't mean that you can't.

One person's idea of success can be very different to somebody else's. Someone may feel that working in a career they love is their ultimate goal. Someone else may describe success as having the freedom to travel the world. Whatever your vision of success looks like, it could be easy for you to achieve. Many of us tend to make life more difficult than is necessary. Look around at the natural world that surrounds you. Nature doesn't make life look difficult. Perhaps nature understands the Universal Laws better than we do. Let us take a look at the Laws of the Universe and the power you hold.

Enjoy the journey.

CHAPTER ONE

YOUR HIDDEN MAGIC

"Reality is merely an illusion, albeit a very persistent one."

Albert Einstein.

If you daydream about the life you wish you had, where do you think your daydreaming visions comes from? That conception materializes from deep inside of you. Your subconscious shows you how your life could be, by projecting these images into your mind's eye. The image, thoughts and feelings arise from within. You are being presented with a deep insight into how it could be. Take a look and become aware of the potential inside of yourself. Do any of us really want to settle for less than we actually deserve? This settling for less can leave us feeling unbalanced and maybe dismayed. Most of us are aware of how precious life is and this goes for our own existence as much as anyone else's. Don't let life just pass you by. The image we perceive in a daydream can leave us feeling awakened, even if it is just for a few precious moments before we return to reality. The sensation of emptiness and dissatisfaction afterwards is a sign from you to you. It's a sign that you are not living your life to the fullest. Many of us do not realise the huge importance of these glimpses. We easily put them down to desires that are unattainable. If we can imagine something better, more satisfying, then it is within the realms of possibility that it can be achieved. We should encourage and embrace these moments of inspiration because that is what they are. Your so-called daydreaming is your future potential. The majority of things that you have achieved in life started out as merely a daydream. A desire inside of you that you worked for and accomplished.

Your reality, the life you are living, has been created by you. If you can see something better in your mind's eye, you can achieve something better. It can all be yours. It's literally all for the taking. Perhaps your inner-self has been trying to tell you, 'this is how it's meant to be.' Have you been listening? Perhaps you just shrug it off as just some sort of pipedream that could never possibly occur. No one is more worthy than another. If there's something you desire, something that is not a detriment to others, then there is no reason why you can't achieve it. If others have achieved the things you desire, then it really could be possible for you to actualize them into your own life. Most of us desire very straightforward things in the search for true happiness. There have been people who desired things in life that didn't at that point even exist! These things merely existed in their imaginations and in their daydreams. Through trial and error and an undoubtable belief, some of these visions became reality. These are the creators of the world. They believe anything is possible. Because of this conviction many achieve the seemingly impossible. Without these dreamers we may just still be living in caves, without all the things we tend to take for granted. Electricity, cars, telephones, aeroplanes would not be here if someone didn't believe in their daydreaming. All these achievements started out just as an image in somebody's mind. Are your desires so immense? I'd take a guess that they are not. If man can achieve such amazing feats, then surely the far more basic needs of you and I should be easily attainable.

Are you one of the millions of people who read the Harry Potter books and watched the films? So many have absolutely loved these books, children and adults alike. I was certainly one of them. I adored the books. But what exactly was it that the fans loved so much? Could it be perhaps, the thought that a person could live their life thinking they knew all there was about the world around them, only to find out the remarkable truth, that they did not understand the half of it? That there was far more out there to offer. I think many of us live life like the character Harry Potter. Existing in what is understood to be absoluteness but in actual fact the absoluteness is not quite so absolute. May I suggest that it might be the time for you to start to look at the power that resides in you.

Now you may at this point be thinking that you do know yourself. Perhaps wondering what else you could possibly learn. Perhaps you know yourself to be a loyal friend. Perhaps you know that you are someone who tends to start things but doesn't tend to finish things. Perhaps you know you are a caring parent. Perhaps you know you let fear stop you achieving. Are these beliefs about yourself the truth? Perhaps.

But are they set in stone? Take some time and a deeper look into what you have come to be and what you would like to become. Most of us are aware of who we are but are not aware of what we are capable of becoming. These two things could be two very different things. Time to take another look, don't you think?

We probably haven't met before, but I am still confident that I know a lot about you. I know you are amazing. Do you know that you are amazing? Perhaps you have no idea how amazing you truly are, many of us live our lives being unaware of this. At this moment in time you may have an untapped source of strength and power that you haven't even realised was there. Most of us do not use the full extent of our abilities. Some use more than others, but most of us could improve our lives if we just took the time to look deep inside of ourselves and figure out who we are and who we would like to be.

We are going to delve into some amazing theories and understandings about the power we all have within us. Hopefully providing you with the tools you need to create the life you desire and deserve. We are going to take a journey into you. Into your mind, body and soul and see if you are putting all your potential to great use. It does not matter if you feel you are not the cleverest or the strongest or the most confident person. None of these self-beliefs will stop you as they are all factors you can change. You can change anything that holds you back. You have the ability to achieve so much. If your heart desires it, and you can focus on it, you can achieve it, whatever *it* is.

If your life is not the most amazing, successful and totally outstanding life ever, then you really need to take some time to reassess. What have you got to lose? Do not waste another moment on a not-so-perfect existence, because inside of you are all the tools and all the equipment needed to sculpt an incredible life for yourself. Your potential is immense. You may have learnt to walk and to talk, and so much more, but at some point did you stop learning about yourself? Why do many of us reach a point where we stop investing time on our own self-discovery? Some people have realised how to achieve their dreams. These are the people that we may see as just naturally talented or even just lucky. They seem to achieve success with complete ease. We may feel envy towards these people or even feel that they are just in a league of their own. There is absolutely no reason why you and I should not join this league. We all have the same biological make up as the great people we look up to. Even Albert Einstein reportedly said that he did not consider himself especially clever or especially gifted. He just considered himself to be very curious. Curiosity is an amazing trait.

Do you consider yourself as curious?

Could you become more curious?

I truly hope you can. As children we tend to be so very inquisitive and through this inquisitiveness we learn so much about the world around us and ourselves. If you could become as curious as you once were, who knows what you could learn.

You can become all the things you wish and dream you already were. You can have the life that, deep down, you desire. You have the ability inside yourself to achieve and accomplish anything. Like so many, you need to realise what you actually can do, not what you can't do. The potential you have hiding away inside yourself is ready to be discovered. Let's re-evaluate your life today. Your body and mind could be likened to a magic wand. Desire it…wish it…attain it. But it only works if you know the magic spell. Do you? 'Abracadabra' is actually a Hebrew word meaning 'I create what I speak.' The clue is in the actual magic spell that children use all around the world! How many times as a child did you say 'abracadabra?' without realising what you were actually saying. I would also like to add 'I create what I think' to this as well.

If you don't already have everything you dream of, or are not quite the person you wish you could be, then you need to read this book. Let's use the magic spell together and see where it leads. Exciting times lie ahead. We will look at science and success stories from some of the most powerfully successful people. Before you have even finished this book you will start to see changes in areas of your life that you wanted to improve. It is not difficult. The answer to leading a fulfilled existence is very simple but because of its simplicity most people overlook it. Sometimes we can easily pass by the obvious and simple, because we just think it should be difficult and intense. When we talk about what is probably the most important thing in your life…achieving a happy satisfying one, then we can be forgiven in believing that the answer to it all has to be something very complicated. You don't need to become the Dalai Lama to achieve enlightenment, but you do need to start to understand yourself better and work on that understanding. Strangely enough happiness and success doesn't come naturally, it comes with growth and understanding, but this understanding is something we can all achieve. It is not uncomfortable. It is completely natural. Some of us have been too busy to actually see that we could be missing the point. Who said you should be working all hours just to get by. Who said life has to be hard and then you die. Your life does not have to be difficult and if you truly want something you can have it.

The knowledge about living successfully has been known by some, for centuries. Many old manuscripts and texts discuss the laws of the universe. Some people have even died trying to protect it, as it was believed so powerful that only a selected few should be aware of it. Others felt that in the wrong hands knowledge like this could be used negatively. Anything powerful can be used for good or bad. Books discussing these powers were sometimes hidden for centuries, lots were destroyed. Fortunately for us, no matter how hard people have tried to hide it, the truth will always prevail and the word will be spread. This is your very own guide, it is never too late to learn about the power inside yourself and the laws of this amazing universe. Many people tend to fight life believing subconsciously, if not consciously, that life is a battle and then you die. It does not have to be this way. If you spend some time learning about life and yourself, you can work with this knowledge rather than struggling without it. It really does not have to be an uphill struggle. Let us now take a deep look into you.

CHAPTER TWO

YOUR CONSCIOUS AND SUBCONSCIOUS MIND

Many of us are aware that the natural world is something amazing, powerful and perhaps even magical. Let us now take a deeper look at you. Let us see if you are just as amazing, powerful and magical. Let us take a moment to have a look at your mind – a deeper understanding here will help you immensely in the whole process of growth and achievement.

Your mind is made up of what we call the conscious mind and the subconscious mind. These do not exist in literal terms. Rather, they are merely labels we use to describe their two different processes. The conscious mind controls logical thinking and the reasoning of situations. Anything we choose to do with intention uses the conscious mind. If I am about to pick up the cup next to me to take a sip of tea, it is my conscious mind that helps me with this process. All thinking and acting whilst awake is due to this part of ourselves. It is also known as the gatekeeper as it filters information received, into things we accept or do not accept, based on our pre-existing belief system.

The subconscious mind controls involuntary actions: everything your body does without you needing to give it any thought. It controls your breathing, the blinking of your eyes, the functioning of your organs and so much more. This part of your being also controls emotions – expressing itself through feelings, habits and sensations. If you start to feel anxious or nervous about something without wanting to feel this way, it's all down to your subconscious. Everything you have ever experienced or seen is stored in this part of your mind. When you think of a memory, it gets retrieved from your subconscious and brought into focus in your conscious mind, until you store it back where it belongs. It has complete knowledge of everything that has helped you become who you are today.

The whole point of having these divided minds is to make life easier. When babies are learning new skills such as walking, they intentionally try to walk. They consciously attempt to achieve the task. Over time, as this new achievement is repeated regularly, the know-how of walking is soaked into the subconscious. Once fully infused, they stop needing to consciously think about the whole process of walking. The subconscious helps us to focus on new things and not on repeated tasks. It enables us to learn so much more if we choose, by freeing our thinking mind up from the day to day living. Once you have trained your subconscious, you will unconsciously be driven by that learned behaviour, belief or habit. So, it is very important that the information we learn is positive information which will empower us, not negative information that will hold us back. Take a moment to just let that sink in. Once you have trained your subconscious, you will unconsciously be driven by that learned behaviour, belief or habit. This is a really important point because, unfortunately, a lot of what is soaked into your core is information given by others. Without maybe realising it, parents, friends, teachers and all the people that were around you growing up have helped sculpt who you believe yourself to be today.

That could be a good thing if your network of support as a child was a healthy and balanced group of people that instilled positive growth messages. If it was not, some of the information held deep inside could easily be damaging your life now. Even as adults we can let behaviours that started as just one-offs become habits that we seem unable to break. Most of us know how it feels to have some sort of vice that we seem unable to control. Our subconscious is not intentionally trying to hurt us in any way, it just believes that the messages you have given it, time and time again, are the truth and nothing but the truth.

An example I can give from my personal experience is my slow build up to a habit of drinking in the evenings to relax. For years, I barely touched alcohol. I would only drink at a party or night out, but would never think about drinking at home. Even when I did have a drink, I rarely went overboard; after a couple of glasses of whatever, I would choose to stop. I would happily volunteer as a driver for a night out as drinking held absolutely no charm to me at all. On starting a new relationship with my now husband, I found myself going over for the evening to his house and taking a bottle of wine along.

It seemed like the polite thing to do, and we would enjoy a meal or film with the wine. Whenever he came along to my home, he also would bring wine. Eventually we moved in together and this tradition of evening wine drinking carried on – it had become an ingrained habit. We would say things along the lines of 'we need a glass of wine to relax' – and our subconscious took this as true. If we had a night without wine, we found that we couldn't properly relax as we no longer knew how.

Logically, I knew that this was not a healthy habit. Consciously, I would decide to take a night off wine, but by the time the evening arrived, I would find myself automatically resigning to that behaviour once again. If you have a weight problem, or any other habit which you would rather not have, I am sure you can relate. You may be extremely unhappy with your weight for example, and logically know what it takes to lose weight, but find that you cannot seem to control the amount of food and the sort of food you eat. This is down to the fact that you have convinced your subconscious that you just cannot resist chocolate (or whatever your issue is.) When I looked at the way I spent my evenings, I knew that I wanted to change my habit of using alcohol to relax. This lack of control is a lack of control from your conscious mind, but total control from your subconscious mind. For me, my subconscious believed that I 'needed' to have wine to relax in the evening. I'd said it enough times, and It believed it was true because this behaviour is one I repeated enough for it to take over and become an automatic response. Whenever I used willpower to refrain, I was left feeling uncomfortable, like I was fighting a battle. And this is exactly what I was doing. My conscious mind and my subconscious were battling, and believe me, the subconscious is far stronger. Fortunately, there are ways to change even the most deeply engrained behaviours and habits. There are ways to become the person you want to be. No matter what story became your reality, you can rewrite your book!

You may have completely different habits that you wish to alter. You may want to build up qualities in your personality or get rid of flaws that are holding you back. You may want more money and to change your 'always financially struggling' mindset to one of abundance. I am here to tell you that it is all possible, and I will show you how easy it is to achieve. Whether you want more money in your life, a better career, better relationships, improved health or something else, it can all be yours. A new version of your life can be scripted as easily as the one you are living right now. It is just a case of looking into yourself to see what you want to change in order to achieve your dreams. Your problem may be smoking, drinking, over-eating, lack of confidence, lack of willpower or maybe something else entirely, but whatever you try, you still struggle with that problem. You can be helped. Your story has been scripted and now you are living through that story. You may have a deep feeling inside that you will never achieve much in life. This belief has stemmed from failures in the past. You may feel that you will never have much money because that is what you have always known. Perhaps you have had money but went and lost it. These beliefs are in your subconscious and have designed the life you have right now. If you have always believed that you will never have the confidence to go and chase your dreams, then you will never have the confidence to go and chase your dreams unless you change your beliefs.

Take the time now to figure out the beliefs you have deep down that hold you back. Become aware of them and then write them down. For this to work, you need to realise what it is that you have believed for years that may be restricting you. Once you have a list of your restrictions you can easily work on changing them. These restricted thoughts and beliefs are what you will be working on. By working on improving these thoughts and beliefs, your life will improve. It goes hand in hand. As you change a belief, you will see the result in an improved area of your life. So, what beliefs would you like to change and how would your life look if you could change them?

For some of us, we live a life feeling trapped in a body, with behaviours and traits that hold us back. The traits and behaviours that are stopping you from living your life to the absolute maximum have been residing in you for as long as you can remember. Understandably then, you may believe that these traits make you who you are and that nothing can change that. But something can change that…you can change that. You are a person who can develop the qualities you desire within yourself. Just by understanding how to work with your subconscious, you can look at all of the elements inside of yourself that you wish to improve, enabling you to mould the life you want. So go on. Grab a pen and paper and get writing. You need to know exactly what you are dealing with. What do you feel needs to change for you to improve?

SUMMARY

- Your conscious mind determines your actions.
- Your subconscious mind determines your reactions.
- You are driven by learned behaviour, beliefs and habits.
- You need to work with your subconscious to change habits, beliefs or behaviours that are holding you back. Time to reassess.
- Control from your subconscious can lead to lack of control of your conscious if the two are not working together.
- Become the person you truly want to be to live the life you desire.

CHAPTER THREE

WHAT ARE YOU MADE UP OF?

"Never mind what-is. Imagine it the way you want it to be so that your vibration is a match to your desire. When your vibration is a match to your desire, all things in your experience will gravitate to meet that match every time."

Abraham-Hicks

By now you should have written a list of your beliefs and the behaviours that you would like to change, or at least have an idea of them in your mind. We will look at how to go about changing them further in this book. But first, let's take a look at what you are actually made up of, in order to get a deeper understanding of who you truly are. Scientists have discovered that everything in our universe is made up of pure energy, including YOU. Socrates believed this theory way back, and it is now becoming accepted by scientists of today. Quantum physics explains that if we take a close look at an atom (which we are all made up of) in a microscope, that there is nothing to actually see – there is only pure energy. These energy waves can be measured and the effects of them seen. Each atom has its own distinct energy frequency or vibration. This vibration is an important factor in how you can go about improving your life.

Multiple Nobel prize winning physicist Niels Bohr has explained that what we see as a physical material world is actually not physical or material at all. Each atom radiates its very own unique energy signature. His theory therefore concludes that you are really a being of energy and vibration, radiating at your own personal level. If you are wondering what all of this scientific information has to do with improving your life, believe me, it has everything to do with it. Your personal level of frequency effects the quality of the life you are living today. The higher your level, the more amazing your life can be. If your frequency is low and you are dissatisfied with your life in any way, your frequency vibrations could be the explanation.

You may already be aware of the law of attraction, where you use the power of belief and your mind to attract the things that you desire into your life. The law of vibration is just as important, despite not being as well-known. To strengthen your chances of a successful life, whatever successful means to you, the two laws need to be used in conjunction with each other. For those who have tried to use the law of attraction and not received the desired results, your personal vibrations could be to blame. No amount of desiring a wonderful life will bring this life about if your frequency is wrong. By tweaking your own energy frequency, amazing things can happen. I will talk further on the law of attraction in a later chapter as there is no doubt that it is a force that we can use for our benefit. Do not worry at this point if you are unaware of the law of attraction as I will explain it thoroughly, as well as the correct method to use to get the most out of this natural law.

For now, let us look at our energy frequency. Raising our energy frequency is not only possible, but easily done. To achieve the most successful life attainable, you need to not only be aware of it, but also to understand how to raise your vibrational level easily and comfortably. Everything has a moving, bouncing energy frequency. A solid rock is not so solid when looked at much closer. All natural things we perceive have a flowing energy. We are all connected to each other, and to everything around us, through these vibrations. We may all have this in common but what differs is the actual vibrational frequency given off – this is the important aspect that we need to consider.

For some, this concept may be hard to grasp. Most of us are aware that science is constantly developing, and regularly bringing us new knowledge and understanding. At first, new concepts may seem implausible, but given time, some of these theories are proven correct. The theory of energy vibration has been around for centuries, even if only recently proved true. Socrates suggested that we were merely energy vibrations as far back as circa 470 BC. Advancement in technology means we are able to see further afield. The natural force I am writing about is not new in any way; yet it may just be a new concept to some. Growing up, I had many experiences that did not seem to make sense. Because of these experiences I started to feel that there could be more to learn about the world around us and about ourselves. I strongly felt that there was more to who we are than originally meets the eye. The next incident I discuss is one of these circumstances. I believe we have all experienced occurrences like this but many of us just write them off as coincidences. But, what if they are not coincidences at all, instead glimpses of powers and strengths that we may not realise that we possess?

When I was a young girl, my mother was very excited about a gift she had just bought for someone. She was excited because of the unusualness of the gift, and asked me to guess what it could be. As soon as she asked me to guess, I actually saw in my mind's eye, a little glass mouse with a coin in it. Before really thinking about this image, I just blurted this rather strange vision out. My mother stood rather shocked. It was in fact, a glass mouse with a half-penny coin in it. Half-penny coins had just stopped being used as currency in the UK. I had never actually seen one of these ornaments before, but it was a crystal-clear image in my mind. How could I have possibly known this? How did I see it in my mind? We were both rather stunned with what just had happened, but since we were both there, there was no denying it. Perhaps it could be classed as some form of psychic power, but I believe it is something far simpler than that. I also believe that we are all capable of it. We are born with capabilities that we use and understand. We are also born with capabilities that, for many, are under-used. As with many things in life, if we do not use it, we lose it. However, when we come to realise that we have strengths and resources that can be fine-tuned, our personal capabilities can grow.

As it is now being shown, even thoughts are energy waves. My mother was thinking about the glass mouse as she asked me to guess what she had. I believe I saw her thoughts in my mind from the vibrational energy that her thoughts had been projecting. Before I had time to doubt myself, I said the first thing that came into my head. I believe that doubting ourselves is the reason most of us have lost the abilities that we were born with. This occurrence reminds me of a film you may have seen called The Matrix. In this film, there is a scene where a man is looking at some computer monitors. On these monitors are moving sequences which I can only really describe as visible white noise. The man watching these screens had trained himself to see real life images out of these moving sequences. He could see people going about their day to day life where the rest of us could not. Perhaps we all see the world in a restricted, blinkered manner. If we could enlighten ourselves, maybe we would even be able to see the vibrations and energy that continually surround us. I think many of us feel these vibrations even if we cannot see them.

I am sure you have had the experience of meeting someone for the first time, and instantly feeling uncomfortable with them for no obvious reason. Or perhaps you have experienced the opposite, when you instantly feel comfortable with someone you have just met. Why is it that we can feel comfortable with some people but not with others before any real interaction has occurred? Could a person's energy frequency have anything to do with this perception? When the energy vibration that you are giving off is similar to that of someone else, you will automatically feel comfortable in their presence. You can tell a lot about someone by the friends they surround themselves with, as often, the people we are close to are very similar in frequencies. There are times in our lives when we find ourselves drifting apart from people who we have been friends with for years, with no reasonable explanation. This is because our energy frequency can alter. The vibrations are not set in stone for our whole lifetime. If either person's vibrations change then relationships can start to feel uncomfortable. It is a disagreeable feeling that we are unable to really understand. We can be left with a friendship or relationship that starts to fall apart. We may not be able to quite put our finger on it, but we can certainly feel it – that gut feeling. The feeling that it is just not what it used to be. Frequencies can go up as well as down. Meeting up with a friend on an equal level leaves us feeling happy after being in their presence. Meeting up with someone with a different frequency can leave us feeling out of sorts. We should always take into account how we feel in the presence of somebody. Trust those gut feelings because they are probably correct! This is a gift we all have, but for many, it is a fairly unused gift, this inner sense we experience gets overlooked. Becoming aware of how we are left feeling after being with somebody should be acknowledged and listened to.

Historically, we were probably more in tune, and used this ability to protect ourselves from harm. Most of us ignore the feelings we get deep down in situations and this can have devastating results. Do not ignore these feelings as they are part of your basic protective make up. We tend nowadays to use only five senses to help us make judgements. In the animal kingdom, this is different. Animals don't warm to people because of how they look. They do not take into account how pretty someone is or how well dressed. They trust an instinct – an animal instinct. Dogs can take an instant liking or disliking to somebody. They rely on an energy frequency. This is something they feel about a person rather than what they see or hear. For many of us, this is an under-used sense that we could all benefit from becoming more aware of, as well as working on raising our own frequency to the highest possible vibration.

Can you imagine how different the route of our lives could have taken, if we were hyper aware of gut instincts. The mistakes that could have been avoided if we had only picked up on vibes beforehand. Sadly, for many, we register these feelings a little too late. After an incident we can feel that deep down we knew something was not correct beforehand but it is a little late to admit this after the event. Our lives could acquire a much more favourable result if we could allow ourselves to develop these insights and then make use of them. Trusting these feelings and adopting them to guide decisions we make with confidence, that we have the power within ourselves to judge situations on an intuition.

So to live the most prosperous and fulfilled life possible entails having the highest vibrational frequency. So, you need to raise your own personal vibration. Once raised, you will be in a powerful position to attract the magnificent life you deserve. We all have our own frequency which attracts similar frequencies. As they say, 'Like attracts like.' An example that affirms this is when you just have 'one of those days!' As soon as you get out of bed it starts and then as the day progresses it goes from bad to worse. You just want to start the day again. The day starts on the wrong foot and then your frame of mind is negative. If you do not just shrug this off, then your day can go from bad to worse. Watch your thoughts. Yes, bad things will happen from time to time but don't make the situation worse by wallowing in them. If you do, then you will certainly have lots to wallow about! We have to accept it, when life throws something negative at us, rise above it and move on. If you can do this, then you will see that life has far more positives for you than negatives. Nobody's life will flow with just positive experiences. Light always follows dark. We are all likely to experience bad situations, but the important factor is how we deal with these situations. Watch how you behave and react. You can make situations worse or not so bad by just thinking correctly. If you deal with the issue in hand and then move on, instead of going around in circles feeling cross at your bad luck, the incident will be far less damaging. You have the ability to choose how you react to things so choose wisely.

Do not get stuck in a negative rut. We all know people like that. It doesn't matter how often you see that person, they tend to constantly be moaning about something or other. When you have been with someone like that, how does it make you actually physically feel afterwards? Probably flat as a pancake. The reason you are left feeling as down as they came across, is not because their personal story bothered you as such, but because their negative energy is surrounding you now. The best thing you can do after an encounter like this is go and take a shower and think of all the great things in your own life and feel those vibrations rise! Sadly, for some people they do not even realise the rut they are in. Drama becomes something they seem to feed off as if that is what life is about. It truly isn't. A person can unwittingly stay stuck in a cycle of negativity, feeding off the concern and kindness shown by others. In the long run though this is a very unhealthy cycle to stay in. The nature of our thoughts and the quality of these thoughts are completely intertwined with our physical reality. Our career, relationships, health etc. depend on the thoughts we regularly have. So our regular thoughts can bring about the standard of life we are living. High frequency thinking can bring about a more abundant happy existence than a low frequency one. Imagine your own level of energy having a range of possibilities for your life. To raise your possibilities for better quality experiences, you need to raise your frequency level. Someone with the lowest form of frequency cannot bring about the best things in life. It just doesn't work. Someone with a low frequency may be left a huge amount of money for example, but if they do not raise their level, then they will very likely lose their fortune. Even if they don't lose it, they are unlikely to achieve happiness and balance even with it.

Have you heard about the researcher and author Masaru Emotu? He has written a book titled The Messages of Water. Emotu's passion is about the magnificence of water, and he has spent years studying it. As we are mostly made up of water, his work is very interesting when it comes to gaining a better understanding of ourselves. Emotu took photographs of frozen water to look at the ice crystals that form. He remembered hearing at school that no one snowflake pattern was alike, and was fascinated by this. He found that the way the crystals formed depended on what the water was exposed to. For example, if beautiful music was played near the water, then when frozen, it created perfect crystal shapes. If loud, angry music was played, the crystals were malformed. He even did tests with words. Positive words created beautiful snowflake shapes but negative words did not!

After hearing about his work, a Japanese school decided to carry out experiments themselves. They had some water which they ignored and did not speak to, water that they spoke positively to and water they spoke negatively to. Positive words like 'love' and 'thank you' created beautiful crystals. The kinder the words expressed, the more detailed the crystals would become. The water that had negative words spoken to them like 'fool' or 'hate' had unformed crystals, as did the water that was ignored. It seems that water itself picks up vibrations and can tell if they are positive or negative. A spoken word or even a thought has a vibration which water sensitively picks up on. Remember that our body consists of mainly water. The average human body is 70 per cent water. It is our life force. If we lose our water, we die. If water is so susceptible to positivity and negativity, then we really should be very aware of our thoughts and, it seems, our spoken words. We may not be able to physically hear vibrations, good or bad, but it seems the water in our body can. As it is being proven time and time again, the condition of our mind has a direct impact on our bodies. Positive, negative and neutral energy is created by the things we say, things we do and the thoughts we have. We create energy every second of every day, and what we send out there into the universe returns to us like a boomerang. Your life situations are equal to your energy vibrations. We can see this on a small scale when we choose to cheer up when we have been in a bad mood. As soon as we decide to make the effort and try, instantly everything around us becomes more positive.

We shouldn't really be surprised that the water in our bodies can be affected from numerous different elements. Many of us already know that the moon can affect human behaviours. There are reports of surgeons who will not perform operations when there is a full moon. Firefighters, police officers and paramedics all over the world have claimed that strange things occur when the moon is full. We know that the moon causes the tides to change because of its pull, so it shouldn't come as a huge surprise that the moon cycles can affect us, too. All of the research by people like Masaru Emoto proves that our bodies are complex things and we should try to be aware of the effects negativity and positivity can have on our lives. Be aware of your thoughts. They could be affecting your frequency without you even realising. Keeping thoughts positive will help raise your vibrations to higher levels. Higher vibrational levels attract a happier life.

Later in the book, we will look into further techniques to raise our personal energy frequencies. So we can have the best outcome possible when we start to use the power of our mind to bring about the life we desire and deserve. There are numerous ways to raise our vibrations, and all of these are easy to carry out. If you incorporate these positive actions into your life, then you will feel the benefit. You will also be in a strong position to bring about the best things into your life.

SUMMARY

- You are a being of energy and vibration, radiating at your own personal level.
- The higher your vibrational frequency, the happier and more successful your life can become.
- The law of vibration works in conjunction with the law of attraction.
- Raising your energy frequency is easily achieved.
- Everything has its own vibrational energy.
- To live the most prosperous and fulfilled life possible entails having the highest vibrational frequency.
- High frequency thinking can bring a more abundant and happy life.
- Think happy thoughts.

CHAPTER FOUR

THE POWER OF YOUR MIND

"Whatever we plant in our subconscious mind and nourish with repetition and emotion will one day become a reality."

Earl Nightingale

You may be familiar with the many powerful and inspiring books on the market concerning the power of our own thoughts. If you have taken the time to read these wonderful pieces of work you possibly have even tried to make some positive affirmations yourself. Perhaps saying things regularly along the lines of, 'I am rich,' 'I am extremely successful,' or 'I am slim and healthy.' For those of you that have, I would like to ask you some essential questions.

Did it work?

Did your positive affirmations turn into actual truths?

Does everything you request from the universe actually come flooding into your life?

Can the process of positive affirmations alone bring about all you desire in life? I believe that positive affirmations are great and immensely powerful but I also strongly believe that we cannot just wish for something, then just expect it to occur. My garden will still need weeding no matter how much I affirm it. If you have believed and stated for years that you just cannot resist chocolate, consciously trying to give up chocolate by just saying out loud "I hate chocolate" will simply not work. You have already unwittingly programmed yourself over the years to believe that you really cannot resist chocolate! It would take just as many years to re-programme using only this positive affirmation approach. Positive affirmations alongside other powerful techniques will bring about the changes in your life that you desire. It applies to all the habits, behaviours and beliefs that you have programmed into your mind. Personal success is undoubtedly available to all those who require it, but we need to look at how exactly we go about achieving it.

Your mind is remarkably powerful. Could it be more powerful than anything that exists in this world today? All inventions have firstly been conceived in somebody's mind. Your mind truly is how you conjure up your whole life. Without your mind, nothing that you do in life or possess would exist for you. People admire powerful computers and are amazed at how quick these machines can work things out, but a human mind brought that programming into existence. A mind designed it making lives easier. Without somebody's mind, computers would never have been invented. Computers can only work on information that has been programmed into it by a human. It does not come up with original ideas. It may be able to work at incredible speed but only with information someone has fed it. However, even the most powerful piece of software and computer system could not do the work our brains and minds carry out daily. We have a filtering system that helps us not to be completely bombarded with information. We have a saving of material option and we can also recall information when we desire. We have been given an amazing piece of software ourselves. Sadly, many of us do not appreciate what we have been designed with, and some of us do not put it to good use. Most things in life can be improved upon. New gadgets will only get better and better as time goes on but the human brain is already the best it can be. The only thing that can be improved is how we use it. We can improve our lives by putting what we already have to better use. The equipment is already there, we just need to understand how to work with its full potential. Unlike computers we have the ability to think, and that ability is a massively valuable tool which we need to put to good use rather than bad.

Positivity is absolutely essential in achieving your desires. I am going to show you exactly how to use positivity to bring about your personal dreams and goals. The power of thought has to be carried out correctly. One of the reasons why positive affirmations do not always work is that you are thinking these positive thoughts using your conscious mind. Your conscious mind is not the part of you that shapes your life, it is the subconscious mind that you need to be working with. The subconscious runs your life 95-99% of the time. If you have beliefs tucked away in the depths of your subconscious mind stating for example, that you are always going to struggle financially, no amount of forcible thinking with your conscious mind is going to trigger any deep-down change in that belief. Positive thinking which uses your intentional thoughts will not work. You may say the words daily but you will spend your time behaving and going about your day to day life with the behaviours of someone who will never have that much money. To make real change, and we truly can do this, we need to delve deeper and work on the subconscious level…sound painful? I promise you it isn't and it is something we can all do ourselves. By working on this level, you will be able to easily fine tune the life you live in all the areas you want improving.

To make the deep down changes in our lives we may need to change areas of our personality that are just not helping us. Now, you may well feel that your personality is a part of you. The part of you that makes you who you are today. Psychologists have long debated the issue of personality. William James argued that by the age of thirty a person's personality becomes fixed with no room for change. He referred to it as being 'set like plaster' and this idea certainly stuck like plaster over the years. This view has been held by many until very recently. When I look back, I know that my personality has changed dramatically since I was a child. If I tell people that I was a shy and unconfident child, friends who know me now would probably not see those traits in me today. I can also see huge changes in myself within the last decade and I am a fair few years older than thirty! My husband and I met twelve years ago and we regularly discuss how much we both have changed since the beginning of our relationship. So how about you? Do you believe your personality is set in stone? Becoming aware of the traits that could be holding you back can be the start of an amazing journey into personal growth. You can actively go about the shaping of your personality which is an empowering thought. There is no part of the brain that has been designated as the seat of your true self so let us take time to develop the self that will best bring about your happiness and success.

Being able to actually think is one of the most powerful tools anyone can have. We are all able to do this but the concept of thinking can differ from one person to another. Some of us will see pictures in our head when we think about something, others may hear their thought in their mind and for some a feeling occurs when thinking. When I ask you to picture or see in your mind's eye, please don't worry if you can't actually see anything. Use the concept of thinking that comes naturally to you. So with this in mind, picture your life how you would like it to be. Take some time to see the details clearly in your mind's eye. Is the picture forming in your mind equal to what your reality is? Are you close enough or are they worlds apart? Don't forget we can change the elements necessary to build the bridge from where you are standing right now to the desired destination. Nothing can stand in the way of your dreams if you don't choose to let it.

Your mind plays an extremely important role when it comes to achieving goals, whether they be small goals or substantial ones. Many of us have smaller day to day goals, but to achieve the best out of life you need to build defined goals for the life you want to live. So many focus on day to day issues like making sure there's food on the table and the bills are paid but don't take the time to consider the bigger, more important elements. To really achieve the happiest, most fulfilled life, you need to use the power of your mind. The way to do this is firstly to get a clear defined goal for the bigger picture of your life. This will require some very serious thinking and investigation. It will take time but time well spent. Don't spend your life just drifting, believing it will all just fall into place. Think of goal developing, like a ship. If the ship has a crew and they all know the destination that they are heading for, the chances are high that they will reach their objective. The journey may be a tough one but with the desired place clearly known they are still highly likely to reach the journey's end. Now, if we took another ship with a crew that did not know the desired destination, what do you think the chances are that they will arrive at the desired journey's end? Unlikely? Successful, happy people know exactly what they want in life. If you ask people out on the street, 'What's your goal in life?' many would not know and those who come up with an answer will probably say something along the lines of 'To survive.' If you find a successful and driven person, the chances are that they could tell you all of their goals immediately. They don't leave it up to chance. They know what they desire in life. Their goals are at the forefront of their mind at all times. So, once you know exactly what you want to accomplish, be sure to keep those desires in your mind constantly. Use that extraordinary imagination of yours and get a clear visual image of how achieving those goals will look. You may feel that holding visions or thoughts in your mind of your desires will be exhausting but it is not. Most people have thoughts running through their mind constantly but unfortunately people tend to use their imagination to picture negative scenarios in their head. Your imagination is a powerful tool. Use it wisely and do not waste it. Use it for what it was intended for. Feed that amazing mind of yours with the images of the life you are after. If visualizing is difficult for you, find physical pictures of the things you would like to have in your life or how you would like your life to look. Look at those pictures and then close your eyes and see them with your mind's eye. Use positive affirmations alongside your visions. These images and affirmations will sink into your subconscious over time and consequently will affect your behaviour and actions. When your subconscious knows where it is it is meant to be heading, situations will occur as they always do, but you will find that you will automatically make decisions and behave in ways that will take you towards your goals. The path will be more clearly defined when you know exactly what it is you ultimately want to achieve.

To achieve your life's desires, motivation has to always be high. To keep motivated you need to think about your goals often. You know how it is when you initially decide on something. Nothing can stop you, it is all you think about. Over time you stop thinking about that goal as often and as you stop thinking, your motivation starts to fade with it. Motivation is important and motivation will stay if you keep focused. See how your desires will affect your life. If your goal is to be fitter, keep the enthusiasm by understanding how being fitter will change your life for the better.

Thoughts as we have already seen possess power. Pour your mental energy into the same thoughts and they will in turn become stronger and stronger. Your attitudes, behaviour and your actions will be positively affected. As thoughts are energy vibrations, others will be able to perceive the vibrations you are putting out there. Especially those people with similar frequencies. You will find opportunities coming your way that were not there before. Suddenly you will meet people or the ideal situations that can help you to reach your goals. What we often term as coincidence may not be coincidences at all. These incidents may occur because of the natural laws of our universe. You have had proof that this happens, I am sure. Have you ever found yourself thinking about someone that you haven't seen for some time, only to then hear from them out of the blue or bump into them on the street shortly after? The universe holds a magical power. I believe that although we may not quite know how we are going to achieve our goal, the universe will pick up on the vibrations of our thoughts and bring about situations that will enable those goals to occur.

I remember renting a house when I started working as a childminder. I was wanting a bigger property to run my business that would suit the needs of both my family and my business. My daughter was just about to finish University and wanted to get somewhere to live with her boyfriend but obviously at this point she did not have a job. I was constantly thinking about this need and started to look for properties. One major drawback was many landlords did not like the idea of a tenant childminding from their home, which obviously narrowed down my possibilities. My estate agent had taken me to view a house which I thought was okay, but just before my husband and I were going to view it together, I received a phone call. A man had just put on the market a four bedroomed property to let in the area we were looking at. It also had a ground floor flat in the basement. His wife had been a childminder for years from the property so he had no issues with me running the same business from there and the rent was only £50 more per month than the much smaller property we were living in! I could not believe it. We were the first to view it and signed there and then. My daughter set up home with her now husband downstairs until they were in a position to look for something more ideal for the pair of them. That property was everything I could of possibly desired and I believe it came about because I had a clear view of what I wanted. It was in my mind continuously. We even moved in the April, which stands out in my memory because for the six months that I was visualising a move, I always pictured us doing so in the Spring.

I believe without any doubt that if you are clear about what you want in life, you do not need to know exactly how you are going to achieve it. Trust the Universe to show you the way. On this note I want to add that you shouldn't even try to figure out exactly how to reach your goal. Have a clear vision of what the end result is that you desire but do not be rigid on how you see that coming about. You do not want to be telling the cosmic force how to do its job. Let it work out how to get things to you. Just be open to see when the opportunity reaches you. If you work out every detail, then you may miss out on an even better opportunity than you could have possibly ever conceived. Be sure to really focus on the desired end result, and do not worry about the steps needed to achieve it. When the steps do come your way, be ready and do what is necessary at that point. So, for example, you may initially think 'I want more money.' Ask yourself what you want that money for. Perhaps it is to be able to buy a house. In that case, the real desire here is to own your own home. So your focus here should be aiming towards owning your own home as opposed to making more money. It is the universe's job to figure out how you will achieve your desire. If you are someone who hasn't had that much in life it may be very hard for you to conceive the amazing possibilities out there, so you could be narrowing the opportunities down by being too precise. Your job is to keep focusing and looking out for when those opportunities arise and grab them as soon as they do. Not all thoughts will be turned into reality. Having a one off thought will not suddenly bring it into existence. Thankfully the thoughts need to be repeated regularly. I mentioned earlier that it is our subconscious we need to work with to get the best results from new desires, and further along I will show you exactly how to go about this.

SUMMARY

- Your subconscious can disregard your new intentions.
- Positive affirmations are great but we cannot just wish for something and then just expect it to occur.
- Our conscious mind is not the part of us that shapes our lives, maybe it is the subconscious mind that does.
- Spend time to investigate what your desires are.
- Use that imagination of yours and get a clear visual image of what your life will be like once you reach your desires.
- Images and affirmations will sink into your subconscious and consequently will affect your behaviour and actions.
- To keep motivated you need to think about your goals often.
- Pour your mental energy into some thoughts and, in turn, they become stronger and stronger.

CHAPTER FIVE

THE SCIENCE OF INTENTION. MAKING THE CHANGES YOU DESIRE

"Most of us attract by default. We just think that we don't have any control over it. Our thoughts and feelings are on autopilot, and so everything is brought to us by default."

Bob Doyle

Intentionally using positive thinking and making regular affirmations to bring change into a person's life has been discussed and believed to hold some form of power by many people, since the beginning of time. It has many names, the law of belief, law of attraction, law of intention, law of the universe and the law of creation. In the East those who are familiar with the laws of attraction understand that mere affirmations will not bring into your life the things you desire. Merely repeating 'I am wealthy in all areas of my life' will not make this real. Saying things like 'I am not in debt' and visualising wealthy conditions in an effort to change present situations, only gives someone a false sense of security. Working with the laws of nature is a powerful act but we do need to assure we are doing it correctly. Misunderstanding of this law by many have left people dreaming their life away. Dreaming away in the hopeless belief that these positive affirmations are enough. There has been a huge false impression about the Eastern and mystical conceptions about the laws of psychological consciousness. We should not deny the negative aspects that exist in our life. We do need to accept the matters in our life that we are unsatisfied with, to enable ourselves to work at changing them. If you have personally tried affirmations in the hope that this law of attraction would work for you, then perhaps you have been left feeling frustrated when all your desires in life still haven't been obtained. Let me go through with you how exactly you can use these natural laws to your full advantage without any misconceptions. You are creating the world you live in right now, and the life you lead, from the thoughts that you allow to develop in your mind. Without intentionally realising it, we are all doing this, all the time. The magic formula here, is to learn to become aware of these thoughts. Form your thoughts and control your thoughts. It basically comes down to control and awareness. Don't be sloppy with your thoughts in the belief that what goes on in your head doesn't matter, because that couldn't be further from the truth. There are some people who use this power of intention to a much more potent effect than others. These wise people realise that being intent on their thoughts can bring a power to them that is literally out of this world. Men and woman have used the power of their own thoughts to achieve health, wealth and happiness for centuries. The knowledge of the power created by ones' own thoughts have been passed through the ages. Some of the most amazing minds like Plato,

Edison, Einstein and so many more have understood the power in themselves, the power that is created by their own thoughts. In manuscripts dating back to ancient times this natural law of the universe, has been understood to be the secret of life. If you haven't been aware of this secret or haven't taken advantage of it, then you are missing out on something profound. By changing your thought patterns to more positive, more intent thoughts, you will start a process to improve elements in the life you are living. Words hold a power. We understand this when we see how happy or hurt someone can be by words spoken to them. Thoughts are just as powerful. Just because they are not spoken out loud does not mean they lose the strength of the spoken word. They are still heard by your subconscious.

We are all subject to the natural and spiritual laws out there. The possibilities are amazing. We must follow these laws correctly however, to ensure they work and not try to bully them. Co-operation with these natural laws is essential. Health, happiness, abundance and success can come from this fusion. There is a difference between focusing intently on a dream and focusing intently on building that dream into reality. Focus intently and do the necessary small steps. This is a very important part. Many people who hear about the laws expect the universe to do all the work. They believe that just thinking about their dream life is enough. It is not. Opportunities will come your way, perhaps unexpectedly but when they do you need to be ready to seize them and then help yourself and work for that dream. There is no need to worry about the exact route you must take in order to create the things in life you desire, just take the opportunities that come your way, keeping in mind at all times the desired end result that you are after. If for example I want to be an author and would like to work full time on this ambition, I don't worry about exactly how I'm going to achieve this. I don't focus on whether I can get published or if I can make a living out of writing. I focus on writing and think about it constantly. I start on the project and then because my intentions and visions are intent and clear I find that new material, new ideas and new knowledge come my way from all types of directions. Even sleep brings me inspiration. I wake in the night with a brilliant idea that excites me. It does not matter where the ideas come from they will come to you. The universe and your mind will bring the answers but only if the universe and your mind know exactly what you are wanting to achieve. Once they do you need to grasp them and work with them. It is not just going to happen without any effort from yourself. You will be given a helping hand when you do, you need to recognise it and put it to good use. As the saying goes 'God helps those who help themselves.' Now you do not need to be religious or to believe in God but there is a power that comes to those who intently focus and try to achieve their life's desires.

Another area concerning the power of attraction, that regularly is carried out incorrectly is down to the actual things people desire. Many people would say they want more money in their life. But most of us don't actually want money, we want money for a certain reason. That reason is what you need to be focusing on, not the money itself. I may say I want money and when pushed for the reason why I want that money, it could become clear that I would like to buy my own home. That home is the real aspiration. That is what I should be focusing on intently. Do not try to do the job of the universe by telling it how to go about it. When you think about what you want in life, think about what you really want. That is the ultimate goal. Then focus on that. We do not always see the opportunities in the restricted view of life that we may have. Be open and you may get what you want in an unexpected way. By being too specific on how you believe you can reach that goal you could be restricting opportunities that you could never have even imaged.

You may struggle to truly accept that your regular thoughts hold such a power and that your life could be altered so massively because of them. Many of us know about gravity and magnetic force even if we don't fully understand it. The universe exists and survives because of these forces and they are part of you as well. Like a magnet every state of consciousness that you have, creates a force which pulls towards you the things in life you desire. Peoples' moods are affected by the phases of the moon. This is a magnetic force. There are other forces in the universe that are just as powerful. The force of attraction is one of them. It is out there and all around you but you need to start to look out for the possibilities that come your way and be ready to act when they do.

Your amazing mind has the knowledge of all. It has the ability to remember everything you have ever heard or experienced. If we were aware of all this information at all times, it would be too overwhelming. Your mind filters out information that your subconscious deems unnecessary. The information we do receive, becomes our personal reality. So if you focus on achieving a certain dream your brain will start to allow information to come your way that will be useful in achieving that desire. If you do not focus on your desires, then all the information that could help you achieve great successes will pass you by. It will still be out there but you won't be aware of it. By focusing intently on all your aspirations then the power of your universe will bring about the information you need to achieve. You will meet the people that could help. You will find the books that will teach. You will gain all the knowledge necessary. I am sure you have experienced this. Think about a time when you bought a certain make of car for example. You think about this car as you choose to buy it. It becomes the focus of your attention. You may talk about it to your friends. All of a sudden you start seeing that model of car everywhere you go. You notice them in carparks when you've been shopping. You may have been unaware of that model until you started to focus on it. This car becomes part of your world and reality because you are now intently tuned in to it. This is the same if your desire is to be able to make more money in your life. If you are focused on that intently you may find an idea come your way that will bring that extra income. But remember, you then have to do what it takes to create it. You will be given the tools and the journey may be an unexpectedly easy one, but you still need to do whatever is necessary.

Visualisation is a tool that will guide you towards these changes. You may already use visualization in your life to help achieve your dreams and if so that is absolutely fantastic. Let us see if we can take this a step further and visualise into place other parts of you that you wish to develop. If you do not purposefully use visualization in your life at the present time, then I honestly hope I can convince you that to achieve anything in your life, visualization is one of the best ways to guarantee it becomes a reality! Countless interviews with successful people show that the one thing most have in common is the use of visualization. Visualisation to see their dreams before those dreams actually become reality.

One very famous story involves the actor Jim Carey. In the early 1990's Jim Carey was an unknown struggling actor. He decided one day to write out a cheque for himself for $10 million for 'acting services rendered.' And he dated this cheque for the year 1994. He kept this cheque in his wallet to help visualise his goal and keep him motivated. Every time he opened his wallet he saw this goal reminder. In 1994 Jim Carrey learnt that he would receive $10 million for his role in Dumb and Dumber. Jim Carrey is now one of America's top movie stars and he credits his 'constant visualization' with helping him to achieve his personal goals.

In areas of sport, visualization is a very common tool used by athletes. If it didn't work why do so many use it? Why do so many coaches teach their athletes the power of this simple process? Arnold Schwarzenegger believed in the power of visualization to help him reach his personal bodybuilding goals. Schwarzenegger uses these same tools to achieve all his life goals. He used a role model in his mind to focus on, and pretend to be. He basically 'faked it until he made it.'

If this is such a powerful and natural law, why doesn't everyone use it? Here's the problem. Most people spend their time thinking about the things they do not want in life rather than what they do want. The magnetic power that is emitted from your thoughts does not understand the negative side…the, 'I don't want.' All that is put out into the universe are the thoughts you think about the most. The law of attraction gives you exactly what you think about the most. If you think about something negative, that is what you will probably attract more of. If you think about not wanting to be ill, for example, then what you will attract is ill health. The way to receive health is by thinking of health not illness. Our thoughts can become actual things. You probably know someone who tends to have bad, unhealthy, romantic relationships. Perhaps you have actually heard them say, 'I always pick the bad ones'? When they think of meeting someone instead of thinking about meeting the perfect person they are thinking about not meeting the un-perfect someone! And time and time again they attract the wrong sort of person. They spend their time thinking and worrying about negative factors and what they don't want this new relationship to turn out like. In the end they are so convinced that this will probably turn out as bad as the last relationship that it becomes true. The new date was just as bad as the last one. Then they are left saying all over again, 'I always pick the bad ones.'

Look at the life you have right now. This may not be what you want from life but it is partly a reflection of your past thoughts. People who think about wealth and abundance as if it is naturally theirs, tend to receive it! Look at some of the worlds millionaires. Most have at some point had business's that failed, but they then are able to rebuild their fortune once again. This is not because they are just damned lucky. It's nothing to do with luck. It's all to do with intention. They believe it. Once they got their millions, the first time around, perhaps they got scared of losing it and focused on that. Once lost, they then start thinking about gaining money again, in a positive light and they build it up again. How many lottery winners have there been, that have won millions to then go and lose it all? Once won they still kept their thoughts of being poor. They did not have a millionaires' mind set. They did not change their thoughts and were scared of losing it and guess what? They lost it. The same goes for people who lose weight, only then to put it all back on. If you do not start thinking thin thoughts instead of thinking fat thoughts, then the weight will more than likely pile back on.

For your intention to work, you do need to realise what you are focusing the most on in life. What thoughts do you spend most of your time thinking about? If there is something you wish to gain in life, let's say improved health. You will have to work hard at making sure you are thinking about perfect health regularly. The power of belief is very obedient. If you want something, focus on that completely. If you struggle from ill health, then you will know that your thoughts and behaviours are regularly thinking about the negative. You will think about the discomfort you are experiencing, and will discuss it with others. If your health problems are known you will be asked by the people in your life who care about you, how you're feeling today? To gain back perfect health you must stop these thoughts and turn them around to focus on the good health that you have. We tend to think of our body being a permanent structure but our body is in a state of constant change.

If you suffer from a physical painful condition, I realise that believing in good health may seem an unlikely way to attain good health. There are numerous accounts of people with extremely debilitating conditions gaining full health through positive thought. I was born with a condition called a dysplastic hip. This problem was not something obvious or realised until I started to get older. At the age of 41, my consultant decided to operate as the pain was increasing. I was very focused on my bad hip back then. To completely sort my problem, I will need a hip replacement but my specialist wanted to wait as long as possible before carrying out this procedure. So I had a bone graft on my hip instead. This procedure was not successful. After eight weeks of not putting any weight on the joint, x-rays showed that the graft never took and there was a gap between my hip and the bone used to try to graft. Anyone with hip issues will know how painful they can be. Family and friends, obviously concerned, would ask me every time we met 'how's your hip?' My thoughts were always on how painful my condition was and the fact my operation did not work.

I have always believed in mind over matter but hadn't really put it into practice concerning my hip. It was very easy for my mind to always be considering my bad leg as I struggled to walk without a limp. Well-wishers constantly asked how I was feeling and I realised that although I could not change what was physically going on with my hip I wanted to know if I could change the way I felt about it and the pain it caused by watching my thoughts. I stopped discussing my discomfort and would think positively about my condition. When asked about my leg I started saying that it was great and do you know what? It started to become true. X-rays show that physically it is still exactly the same. I will one day need a hip replacement but I am doing everything I want even walking up local mountains! It does hurt sometimes, but very rarely. I don't feel the need to take medication except on the very rare occasion. I have even noticed that I'm not limping. The power of the mind is an amazing thing. Use it for you, or against you, the choice is yours but never underestimate it.

We can easily fall into the trap of moaning about life and discussing all our ailments. If you are someone who finds themselves discussing ill health, take a moment next time you catch yourself and stop. Do not forget that your body physically goes through 7 to 10 year cycles. In a seven year cycle every cell has been replaced, so essentially every seven years we become new people. What a wonderful thought. If you originally grew your body, which you did, why not believe you can renew your health and banish ill-health. We know you had the ability originally to create yourself, so couldn't it be possible to recreate yourself? You can create a physically healthy body and a healthy balanced mind. Your cells actually have an endless life span; could it be your state of mind that ages you? We all know of people who behave far older than their years and others who seem so youthful into old age. It all comes down to their state of mind about age. You do have a choice.

Your skin renews itself every two to four weeks. Your skeleton is constantly replacing itself and takes about ten years to completely do this. Even your heart is rejuvenating. As this has been proven scientifically isn't it acceptable to believe that when ailments arise that with positive belief we could see those ailments disappear? If you know you have arthritis and you discuss it as you feel the discomfort you are sending messages to your subconscious about that pain. Even if the arthritis magically disappeared tomorrow, your subconscious mind would not know this and would still be convincing you of your pain. If on the other hand you excepted that your body is an amazing machine and is renewing itself and you have perfect health your subconscious would start to take this as the truth and you may just find the pain disappears.

Just look at the placebo effect used by scientists and doctors. This has been a technique used for years. The sugar pill is an example of the placebo effect. It is given as a fake medication to patients unknowingly. More often than not, patients still get better. The only explanation for this is the power of their belief that they would get better. They believed they were taking something to rid them of their illness, then because they believed they would be cured, they actually were cured. There are huge amounts of studies into this area to read if you are interested.

Our regular thoughts can become our desire, our desire can inspire us to take action. We can then create the results that we originally thought about. Note the take action part, this is vital for this law to work. When you focus on the life you want you are actually summoning it into existence. My mother did believe in the power of mind when we were younger, however she hasn't always believed in the power of *her* mind. She completely accepted if someone else said that they had strongly pictured something and then attracted it into their lives. She fully believed that was possible. When we were young I remember her saying on more than one occasion, how we always had just enough. Just enough to survive. Just enough to pay the bills. Just enough to cover emergencies. She knew that if a bill came along, something would turn up giving her the resources to pay off that bill. She was right. Every time she received an unexpected expense she always found a way to pay it off. I'm sure my mum thought she was being positive with this mind set. After all she wasn't saying that she would never have enough money. But was she doing herself a disservice? If she believed this to be true…which she certainly did, what would have occurred if she had truly believed in more? Would she of received an abundance of money if she believed it would occur? It would take no extra effort to believe in more money as it did about just scraping by. Sometimes mum would allow herself to believe that she could bring more to herself but here's the key, she would always go back to her original belief. That deep ingrained belief that she would always have just enough. I am not sure if she felt that picturing herself with an abundance would come across as being greedy and I suspect this was the case. Deep down my mother did not believe she was worthy of wealth. In her heart, for whatever reasons, she did not believe it for herself. How sad is that? Why would she be less disserving than any other single mother in this world. Or any married mother, or any other person full stop. Of course she was just as worthy as are you and anybody else. I am very happy to say that this is not the case with my mum anymore. I am pleased to say that she no longer lives like this. My mother's life has turned around since I was a child. She certainly now lives it to the full and certainly believes anything is possible!

> *"You cannot entertain weak, harmful, negative thoughts ten hours a day and expect to bring about beautiful, strong and harmonious conditions by ten minutes of strong, positive, creative thought."*
>
> Charles Haanel

Some of the boundaries that are surrounding you in this life are actually boundaries that you have constructed yourself with your own mind. Things that hold you back from achieving what you would love to be or experience is down to your own belief system. Reasons that you use for not achieving your desires tend to be excuses based from fear which inevitably come from inside of you. If you feel that you could never do that job, because you're not clever or talented enough, then you are creating that reality. If anything has been achieved by others, then why not you? If someone has achieved something, then it certainly can be achieved by you. Even things that have not been achieved yet by anyone, does not necessarily mean it is not possible. If you can imagine it, see it in your mind's eye then it could just be possible. If someone didn't believe in the seemingly impossible, then so many things we now take for granted in our lives just wouldn't exist. Telephones, televisions, aeroplanes, computers…all started out as a thought in some one's mind. To achieve anything, you need to see the completed image in your mind first.

It is believed by many, that everything in our lives has been attracted to us because of the thoughts that run through our head. All could of been attracted to you because of your primary thoughts. Attracted to you because of images you put in your own mind. Remember the subconscious cannot see, so your thoughts are its reality. If you are thinking "I need to lose weight" then you will be attracting the fact that you are overweight. You will also be focusing on the future not the present which means you will never achieve it. That future term, 'I will' never arrives. You are continually reinforcing in your mind that you need to stay overweight so the thought "I need to lose weight" makes sense to your subconscious. We attract like a magnet the thoughts we think. If you don't give attention to the thoughts running through your mind daily, how do you know if your thinking is positive or negative? When you focus on those thoughts, you may see that you are mainly focused on the negative. Take control. If you think that observing your inner dialogue constantly could be difficult I can assure you it isn't. If you are feeling good, then your thoughts must be positive. You cannot possibly feel bad if you are having good thoughts. The opposite is also true, thinking bad thoughts will leave you feeling low. So if you find yourself feeling down or unhappy, stop. Figure out what thoughts you are have running through your mind at that moment and change them. Just watch how your mood will improve once your thoughts do.

SUMMARY

- The magic formula is to learn to become aware of your thoughts.
- Your thoughts matter.
- Men and woman have used the power of their own thoughts to achieve health, wealth and happiness for centuries.
- By changing your thought patterns to more positive, more intent thoughts, better things will start to form in the life you are living.
- The universe and your mind will bring the answers but only if the universe and your mind know exactly what you are wanting to achieve.
- By focusing intently on all of your goals then your world will bring about the information you need to achieve.
- Most people spend their time thinking about the things they do not want in life rather than what they do want.

- This may not be what you want from life but it is a reflection of your past thoughts.

- The power of belief is very obedient.

- When you focus on the life you want you are actually summoning it into existence.

- Visualise your dreams. See them in your mind's eye clearly, to make them reality.

- Fake it to make it.

- We attract like a magnet the things we focus on.

CHAPTER SIX

USING SELF-HYPNOSIS TO BRING ABOUT CHANGES

In the earlier chapter, which discussed your conscious and subconscious mind, I asked you to write a list of your habits and behaviours that you may like to change in some way. Let us now look at how we are going to go about changing these patterns of behaviour. But firstly let us remind ourselves how these undesirable qualities may have come about in the first place. As a child you probably heard remarks made by others concerning opinions about your character. These comments were also perceived by you subconsciously. Over time these comments can be assimilated into our own minds so deeply that we can register them as true observations of who we are.

Fortunately, you have the ability to remove these personal impressions and replace them with more empowering ones. The first stage towards the remodelling of you is to examine the judgements you have that may be holding you back in life. Secondly, you will essentially go about reprograming, to become who you want to be. By substituting beliefs about our characteristics for more positive attributes you will be on the right path to the life you desire. As already mentioned, the most successful way of intentionally altering behaviours and belief systems has to be dealt with subconsciously. But how do you actually go about this when you have a conscious mind guarding the gates? This guard does not want to let information in, information that goes against the grain of your personal in-built beliefs. How can you convince yourself, that you are now, a confident person for example, when you have told yourself time and time again that you are not? How do you convince yourself this when others have told you that you are not? Can you really change that? Starting your day by looking at yourself in the mirror and stating 'I am confident' is powerful. However, we need to do something on a deeper level, something that will work at the core of your beliefs. Beliefs that may have been festering inside for years and over these years building more and more strength. If we do not work on a subconscious level initially, positive affirmations that go against your belief system will just be rejected. We cannot bully ourselves by just shouting it a hundred times a day, 'I am a confident person…I am a confident person.' This will not easily be accepted by your inner self. You need to persuade your conscious mind to take a step back for a while so you can sneak into your subconscious and change some elements that are now holding you back in life.

Using self-hypnosis techniques can bring about real changes to your life. Once your conscious mind has taken a step back, which is exactly what occurs under hypnosis, you will be able to work with the subconscious by using visualization and affirmations. Showing your subconscious exactly how you want your life to be. Showing your subconscious exactly how you want to be. Self-hypnosis might be a practice that concerns people somewhat as 'hypnosis' may have negative connotations attached to it. A lot of people relate it to stage hypnosis where the audience participating in the show seem to have no control of what they are doing. Some people have a fear of trances as it seems to puts them into a vulnerable position as someone else holds the power over their mind. However, all self-hypnosis actually is, is visualizing and making affirmations whilst in a deep relaxed state. Nothing frightening and certainly nothing scary. Once deeply relaxed you will be working with your subconscious mind not your conscious mind. That's it. That is all there is to it. Nothing mystical, dramatic or dangerous. Self-hypnosis is just as wonderful as meditation, but once in that super relaxed state, instead of trying to clear your mind you start purposefully visualizing the things you are after in life. Your subconscious experiences what you are trying to achieve and bring about. If you are someone who loses their temper easily for example, and this is something about yourself that you would really love to change, then in this relaxed state you would visualise yourself as a calm person reacting to situations with self-control. This image in your mind whilst in hypnosis is very powerful and will create changes in your reactions to things. If you are someone who wants to lose weight and be healthy, then in self-hypnosis you will picture yourself looking slim and behaving differently in situations that would usually have you overeating. I say picture yourself, but don't forget what I said about thoughts. You may not be able to visualise. You may just feel it or just think it. It does not matter.

I qualified as a Hypnotherapist years ago so I understand how powerful this process can actually be. But I believe that self-hypnosis is even more powerful. After all, even with a therapist guiding you, you are still the one doing the changes. The power to make changes in your life is all under your own control. Your subconscious mind does not have eyes. Its knowledge comes from you and the regular thoughts you feed it. Working directly with the subconscious gives you a direct route to the inner part of you that makes you who you are. Most of us believe that a child can be moulded by the guidance of those around them. But most of us do not realise that we can still be moulded once we are older. We can make decisions about our personality, character and our behaviours. We can alter the things we would like to change and self-hypnosis is the way to go about this change. So let's take a look at exactly how we are going to do this.

The first part is exactly the same process as meditation. Meditation and self-hypnosis are both extremely beneficial techniques. If you do not already incorporate these techniques into your life, then I would seriously recommend that you start. You are aiming to reach a place where your conscious mind quietens down. A place where the thoughts of the day drift away. When this quietening of the mind occurs your conscious mind will be resting, just like in sleep. Then you can start working on your subconscious; the storehouse of all your memories, all your behaviours, all your traits. The part of you that makes you who you are. Great changes can be had once you're in this place. Once you feel your thoughts have quietened down and you are comfortably relaxed then this is the point that you can start working with the changes you would like to actualize. Do not worry if you cannot stop all thoughts running in and out of your mind. It is very difficult to stop them all. It is normal for the odd ones to appear but when you realise one has, let it go and carry on, clearing your mind of others. You will realise when your state of mind is quieter than before and this is what you are trying to accomplish. Practice will make this process easier. For me personally when I reach this state of relaxation, I find that I see visions of my dream from the previous night in my mind's eye. I may not have remembered my dream before this point but it tends to come back to me whilst in this deep relaxed state. This indicates to me that my brain waves are in a sleep like state whilst I am still awake. This is something that occurs for me but may not everyone. You will learn over time to recognise your personal indications that you have reached a deep enough place to be able to start your visualisations.

So to start, get yourself comfortable in a place where you are unlikely to be disturbed. Either lying down or sitting, whichever you prefer. If you do get disturbed, even when you are in a deep relaxed place, do not worry. It is not dangerous to be woken quickly from hypnosis, it just doesn't feel very pleasant. Just like being rudely awakened from a deep sleep. It is not dangerous but certainly not nice. Just be careful in case you feel somewhat dizzy if interrupted. This will pass quickly. Start by becoming aware of your body. You want to be checking that every part of you is relaxed. Start by focusing at the top of your head and slowly move down your body with your mind making sure that all areas are as relaxed as possible.

If you find you are uncomfortable move your position until you are as comfortable as can be. We can sometimes hold tension in areas of our body that we are not really aware of. Focusing in this way will help ensure that you relax all parts of yourself. Once you have got yourself comfortable, and you have ensured that all the muscles in your body are as relaxed as they possibly can, you are then going to become aware of your breathing. By focusing on one thing alone, other intrusions of the mind will filter out allowing your thoughts to quieten down. Just being aware of that one thing, your breath, will enable thoughts to be pushed out of your minds focus. It may take some time for you to feel that your thoughts are purely on your breathing but practice definitely helps. The more you do this the easier it becomes. Even so, quieting down the thoughts to some extent, if not altogether, can be immensely beneficial. Do not get frustrated if you find yourself drifting back to thinking, just become aware that you have and refocus on your breathing again. Over time you will find that your state of relaxation gets deeper yet it will be valuable from day one. Become aware of every breath out taking you into a deeper relaxed state. Each breathe out will take your level of relaxation even further.

The difference between meditation and self-hypnosis is at this point. Once you have quietened your thinking brain down from everyday thoughts you are now going to purposely visualise and make affirmations. With meditation you just keep the brain as quietly relaxed for as long as you desire. But with hypnosis you will purposefully start to think about specific areas of your life. The areas you wish to work on. Start to think about how you wish your life to look. If you use visual senses easily, you will see this as clear pictures. If you prefer you will just have thoughts about this life or you may hear dialogue. Whatever your natural preference, you are projecting the life that you would like to be living. How you would like it to be, showing yourself what it will entail. Now this could be a fitter version of you or a you with more confidence. Whatever your goal for change is, make the picture in your mind as clear as possible. Some people struggle to see actual images and that is okay, you just need to be thinking the thought that you are trying to create in your life. Think about how you will be once you have achieved your desires. What are you wearing? What are you doing? How are you feeling? The stronger you can feel about this change the better. Work on actually making that desire so real that you can almost feel it. Get excited about it as if it is already real. Emotion is a powerful tool, so use it here intentionally. Your subconscious will be given clear thoughts and images of your goals. Like I have mentioned before, your subconscious mind does not have eyes. Its eyes are the thoughts you pass to it.

Just to prove this point I want you to try now to think about something that would really upset you if it actually occurred. Try to think of one of your deepest fears. Really take the time to feel what it would be like if this fear occurred. Whilst doing this observe what actually happens to your body physically. You may find that your heart rate starts to beat faster. Is your stomach starting to churn and get upset? Are tears coming to your eyes? This is just what occurs whilst thinking about something upsetting. Our body starts to physically react and the reason for this is that your subconscious believes what you are telling it, taking every thought you have literally. This is such an amazing fact for us to understand if we use this knowledge to our advantage. Work with it. Why do we think we get so scared from horror films? I personally cannot watch them. I get so frightened and that fear, irrational as it is, stays with me for days! Consciously we know that we are just sat on the sofa watching a film but your subconscious is taking it in as real.

Whilst in hypnosis do not only visualise life as you want it but also use those positive affirmations we discussed earlier. All those positive statements will be even more powerful said to yourself in this state. 'I am confident,'' I am healthy,' 'I am wealthy' are all more potent suggestions when in hypnosis. Once you have said these affirmations in hypnosis stating or restating them in your day to day life will just go to add to the work you have already started. You plant the desires you want to grow in your life whilst in hypnosis and water them regularly throughout your normal day to see those ideas and desires flourish. The statements you make whilst in a hypnotic state should be positive statements not negative. Your affirmations for the goals you desire should also be stated as if they already have been achieved. For example, losing weight statements should be along the lines of 'I am slim and healthy. I am at a healthy weight.' Be clear about the weight you want to be and make happy statements in your mind that you are already at that weight. The reason for saying these messages in the present is down to the fact that if you say them in the future tense, like 'I will be slim,' 'I will be healthy,' then your subconscious will believe this is something for the future and not for now. And as we know the future never actually happens. The future is never at this moment in time, so think in the now. Always make statements as if you have already achieved your goals. If you keep thinking these positive statements your mind will endeavour to make your statements reality. The saying, 'you need to fake it to make it' is extremely true.

Remember when making these affirmations you need to try and feel emotion alongside the actual thought. You need to feel how it would be if your dreams had come true. Emotion is a powerful thing. We want our body to react as if we have achieved everything we want. If you have ever been healthy and slim, try to think back to the way you felt and remind yourself of that wonderful feeling. This will help your inner mind believe that you are exactly how you want to be. So alongside those positive statements, visualise your goals as if they have already occurred. Picture exactly how you will look as this new slim healthy person. If you find this difficult find a picture of somebody else who is the size you desire, and picture their body being yours. Think about the clothes you will wear and how confident you would behave. Remember, think as if it is your reality now. See yourself with healthy eating habits. Tell yourself the opposite to what you have convinced yourself before now. If you have loved chocolate, tell yourself now that you dislike the taste of chocolate. Picture yourself as a person who has a huge amount of self-control were food is concerned. You are strong and food will never get the better of you. Say statements that tell yourself that it is easy to eat well. Have fun with this. Whilst relaxed just see the life you want. See how you would behave if you had the career you desired. Do you stand straighter with your head held high? What would you be wearing if money was no object? Remember as a child imagination was a great thing. Reclaim it now. Have fun with it. All dreams and ambitions start out in our imagination then we form it into reality.

A very important part of this retraining is that you do not contradict yourself. There is absolutely no point in spending half an hour visualising and making positive statements if afterwards you start to think negative thoughts that go against all you have been programming within yourself. This would be like planting carrot seeds in soil then pulling them out but still expecting carrots to grow! Think of it like ordering from a mail order catalogue. You place the order and then believe it is on its way. You need to believe it with all your might. Once you choose to come out of your deep relaxed state just slowly start to become aware of your body and surroundings. Take your time when you get up and let yourself slowly come round, just as you would after a sleep. Then carry on behaving and thinking positively as if all that you visualized had already come true. As if it is already real. Keep behaving as that slim person or that confident person or that high flying career person. Do the things you know that you would do if it was already real. Don't go back to behaving the way you have always behaved. You need to start changing for situations in your life to change. Doing the same things over and over again will only bring about the same results over and over again. Just like a child playing, let's pretend…pretend. Before long, you will suddenly realise that you are no longer pretending. Realising it is now real!

I will give you an example of how this worked for me. As a child we moved a lot which meant regularly changing areas and schools. Now I hated the school changes because I was a shy child who lacked confidence. At schools I would be bullied and teased regularly because of my meek manner. I literally hated school and would do whatever I could to avoid going. When I was fourteen we moved to Wales and a new high school was waiting for me…again. My new uniform was bought and I remember thinking…no more! I will not get bullied this time or struggle to make friends. I gave some serious thought about the qualities a confident person had and decided to mirror their behaviours. Basically to copy them and pretend. The main image I had in my head was that confident people tend to hold their head up high and look people in the eye. Unlike my usual behaviour of avoiding eye contact at all costs. The first day came and my new form tutor stood me in front of the class to introduce me to the other pupils. Now my natural behaviour would have been to look at my feet at this moment and wish I could escape but I stood there, head held high and purposely scanned the room looking all the students directly in the eye. I went from one face to the next. I was sent to sit down by a girl named Sharon and I spoke to her, asked her questions about herself and answered any aimed at me. We instantly got on. She didn't think I was strange because I wasn't talking, she seemed to actually like me. She even introduced me to all her friends at break time and do you know what? I actually became the popular new girl. Not the scared bullied girl which I'd been before. School became fun for me. I had friends who enjoyed my company. Down the line I told my new friends how shy a person I was and they laughed. They actually didn't believe me. The thing was at some point I stopped pretending I was confident because I actually really was. Still to this day I will tell people about my shyness and no one sees that in me anymore. Since I was young, my shyness had not become so deeply developed as a character trait. I was able to work at changing it purely by deciding to fake it. As we get older these traits become harder to alter and this is when self-hypnosis really helps. My new confident self became my true reality after just playing at it for a very short while. This could be exactly the same for you, whatever it is you are trying to achieve or stop. For more ingrained negative behaviours and habits self-hypnosis will be beneficial. Use it alongside the mirroring of character that you wish you already had, and see how quickly it becomes ingrained as a part of you.

I hope that you can see that self-hypnosis is nothing to be wary about. It really is only a process that allows you to get into a very deep relaxed state. In this place you can work in a much more powerful way. Making changes you desire to your thought patterns, and the seemingly automatic behaviours that you have that have been holding you back over the years. Hypnosis allows you time to take a deeper look at the inner you that holds so much control over the behaviours and character that you show to the outer world around you. Think about it as a chalk board. Over past years of your life, messages about who you are were scribbled on this board. Once on there, these became your reality. Now by taking a closer look you can decide which of those messages are holding you back from reaching your full potential as a person. You can now wipe that board clean and rewrite more useful messages. Messages that will empower you and help you grow in the direction you desire.

SUMMARY

- Meditation is when you are deeply relaxed and your conscious mind quietens down.
- Self-hypnosis is just visualising and making affirmations whilst in a deeply relaxed state.
- With self-hypnosis you can start to purposely visualise images of how you wish your life to be.
- Plant the desires you want to grow in your life whilst under hypnosis and water them regularly throughout your normal day to see those ideas and desires flourish.
- Your subconscious does not have eyes. It ‘sees’ the thoughts you pass to it as real.

CHAPTER SEVEN

RAISING YOUR ENERGY FREQUENCY TO BRING SUCCESS INTO YOUR LIFE

We have already discussed the difference in energy vibration from one person to another. To gain the most in life successfully we need to keep our vibrations at the highest level as possible. In this chapter we are going to look at two essential ways to raise our energy vibration. One way to raise the vibrational frequency, is through the types of food you choose to eat. You are what you eat…you've heard that right? We already know what we should be eating for health benefits but how about the benefits of achieving life's dreams and goals? Usually if we think about food, we are looking at it from the angle of nutrients and physical health. I want you to take a look at food in terms of energy. As we have already discussed, we are all formed from energy, our mind, bodies and even thoughts. Food is also made up of energy so if we are to raise our own vibrational frequency, eating foods high in energy vibration is a great way to start. I believe that high frequencies can bring us a higher quality of life. Not only do some foods fare better when it comes to raising a person's frequency once eaten, but some foods can actually lower frequency. Obviously if we are attempting to enlighten ourselves to the highest possible point we need to be aware of which foods raise and which foods lower.

Science classes discuss photosynthesis; which means plants use light from the sun to produce their energy source. If we eat plenty of food that has the ability to use this magnificent source of energy, we can benefit hugely. We couldn't get a better source of vibrational energy than the suns. The powerhouse of the universe can be our own personal charger. Plug into this amazing source by eating products fed by it. Eating high energy food will help us reach higher consciousness and we can better connect with our higher source. Foods that are highly processed, produced rather than grown, will lower your frequency. Fresh grown food like fruit, vegetables, seeds, beans, grains, herbs and spices will help raise your frequencies. Do not forget that food is alive, and cooking changes a foods state. Try to eat as much raw live food as possible.

Have you heard about kirlian photography? This is a photographic technique that makes energy fields visible around living and non-living objects. It has enabled us to see previously unseen energy fields. There is a huge difference between the energy shown around raw, organic food in relation to cooked food. This photography shows clearly the types of food with more energy radiating from it. Coming out on top is definitely raw organic grown produce. Look it up and see for yourself. It certainly made me more inclined to make a raw fruit and vegetable juice every day!

As well as eating food energised by the sun, spending time outdoors in the fresh air under the sun is also a great way to raise energy. Exposure to direct sunlight for too long is associated with skin cancer, but time outdoors also has many benefits that we may already be aware of. These include mood boosting qualities down to the chemicals created in the brain. It also helps with skin conditions like eczema, psoriasis, acne etc. As well as the benefits we are all probably aware of, time outdoors in the fresh air raises our vibrations.

Another powerful technique you can carry out to achieve balance in your life and build up your energy frequency is meditating. If you do not already practice meditation, then you really are missing out on something extremely beneficial for your health and overall wellbeing. Meditation is one of the best ways to increase your positive energy. With meditating practices, you can achieve a mindfulness that helps bring about growth from within and a deeper personal understanding. The term "meditate" originates from the Latin word meditatum which means 'to ponder.' The practice of meditation dates back to prehistoric origin. Meditation originated in India and forms a part of many religions throughout the world. Although linked to many religions, you do not need to be of any religious persuasion to gain the benefits from this amazing process. Some experts have compared it to a 'reset button' for your body. The time taken in meditation brings about a freshness of the mind and revived energy. Regular meditation will allow your conscious mind to take a step back and just relax. There are numerous benefits to meditating and one of these amazing blessings is the uplifting of your personal energy frequency.

Meditating will also award you with a greater energy level. I find it hard to understand why everyone does not practice this form of relaxation because the benefits are so immense. I know that time is an issue for many. If you feel that you do not have enough time in your life to fit meditation in, then you probably need it more than most. The feeling of calm you achieve after the process is incredible. Layers of negativity, anger, guilt, insecurity, whatever the negativity is, can be cleared away during meditation and an unblocking in the soul seems to occur.

As a child, you may of regularly woke early, no matter how early it was, you probably wanted to get up and enjoy the day. Explore and play. Over the years we can find that the excitement we once felt for a new day dissipates and we are not so keen to see what the day has instore for us. This can be down to the knocks we have had in life. Experiences and incidents that occur over time. Exposure to these things start to block our energy and alter our frame of mind. Even if you cannot really remember ever experiencing a calmness about life, you can be taken to a harmonious state through the practice of regular meditation. A place where you feel less anxiety for the day ahead and excitement to go out there and seize that day. The more you practice the deeper the intensity of relaxation. But even from the very first attempt your body, soul and mind will thank you. I look forward to meditating each day, where I can practice this deep relaxation. It is not like sleeping as you are fully aware of the serene state that you are in. Sleep does bring about relaxation but you are not consciously aware of the actual feeling this relaxed state gives you. With meditation you are.

In our-oh-so busy lives, we tend to get caught up with the habit of just being busy. We run around discussing the fact that there's just not enough hours in the day. We never seem to get a moment to ourselves. From the moment we wake up, most of us have lists running through our head of all the things we need to get done that day. We lose so much energy just in the process of thinking about all the things we are trying to achieve. We seem to have lost the ability to take time to stop for a moment, to quieten our lives and focus on ourselves. By doing this you can achieve so much more in your life as you are fully charged, less stressed and clearer minded. Time taken to relax in this way is never time wasted. To be able to achieve your life's desires, does not necessarily mean you have to always be busy. In fact, the opposite is probably more true. Things can come to you easier than you probably realise. To become wealthy, you do not necessarily need to work more or harder, you just need to become more intent on what you are actually after. Intentions must be clear and meditation helps here massively. Clear intentions and calm minds are powerful forces, to achieve your desires. People can be so busy that they miss the opportunities that are staring them in the face.

If you take some time out of your busy schedule you can actually recharge, so that you achieve more after the process. Meditation can actually help you become more productive. Nothing really gets achieved by chasing your tail. People who regularly use meditation in their lives can be more successful and achieve far more. As well as helping you to recharge, meditation has been proved to help focus the mind. After meditating you become more focused and energised for the tasks ahead. Stress levels lower, leaving your body in a much healthier state. We all know that feeling when our stress levels are so high, when we are so busy that the more we rush the less we actually seem to achieve.

Sadly, for many of us, the importance of just being, and taking care of our mental health is not a priority. However, if you realised the importance of doing this and the massive benefits that can be achieved, then you certainly would fit this practice into your life. We need to remember to take stock of our mental health from time to time. The benefits of doing this are immense. If you are thinking that meditating is not something that could be associated with success, then think again. Some top Fortune 500 companies, like Google, AOL and Apple offer meditation classes to their employees!! These companies understand that meditation improves cognitive functioning and productivity.

> *"Meditation more than anything in my life was the biggest ingredient of whatever success I've had."*
>
> Ray Dalio, billionaire
> Founder of Bridgewater Associates

Meditation is an amazing process of relaxing where for that moment you stop being aware of thoughts and the outside environment and become aware of your internal self. By quietening your thoughts and deeply relaxing whilst still awake you give your body, time to heal itself, destress and re-energise. Whilst in this relaxed state your heart rate slows down and your body becomes deeply relaxed. In deep meditation you can actually become unaware of your body completely as your awareness shifts to your spiritual side. After meditation you will find that your mind is calmer. For many that suffer with hyper behaviours, stress and anxiety, the benefit is massive. The act of meditation can clear away negativity, anger, guilt and so much more leaving you with an inner calmness, confidence and a feeling of deep happiness. You have been given a magnificent tool to heal the damage that your over stimulating life has caused. It is a sad situation, especially in western society, that meditation is not the prescription for our crazily busy lives. We need to learn to heal ourselves. We should empower ourselves by listening to our own personal needs and become our own doctor.

Meditation is a natural act so is very easy to do. It can be done before sleeping at night when you have some time to spare or even whilst out in nature. The combination of nature and meditating is highly beneficial. It can leave you with such an inner sense of peace and an attachment to the beautiful surroundings around you. I am very lucky to live in a beautiful part of the world near the sea and mountains. I try to spend as much time outside as I can. Whilst soaking up the scenery, I will take time to stop my thoughts running from one thing to the next and just focus on my breadth. All you are trying to achieve is the place of not trying to achieve anything. For that moment in time, to just be. To feel the energy that makes up you, mingling with the energy of your surroundings. You can experience a feeling of becoming one with nature.

So to start this deep relaxation find somewhere quiet that you are less likely to be disturbed. Some people like to sit up doing this. If so make sure your head is comfortable so it doesn't roll once you relax fully. I personally like lying down. The length of time you focus in this very relaxed state is totally down to yourself but try and invest as much time in yourself as possible. I personally like to do a long meditation every night. This can take half an hour or more. This is not some sort of chore as the feeling of such a deep relaxation is fantastic and it definitely becomes quite addictive. I look forward to these times. If I am tired and feel like I am drifting to sleep then that is fine. There are no strict rules here.

Once you have made yourself comfortable then close your eyes and try to quieten your thinking mind down. At first, thoughts will be flying around but the object of what you are doing is to quieten those thoughts down. We are able to do this by focusing on one thing. For many people focusing on their breathing is good. With this we are focusing on something internal. Some people feel better keeping their eyes open and focusing on an object. You will need to find what is most suitable for you. For a while you will find thoughts slipping into your mind. Do not stress about it. As you acknowledge the thought let it go and refocus on your breathing. You will find yourself becoming very relaxed and once a deep relaxation occurs you will enjoy how wonderful this state can feel. This may take time to achieve but like most things it will get easier with practice. You can be sure that even from the first time though you will be achieving relaxation benefits. Mediation is one very powerful way to raise your vibrations. For you to get the best out of yourself your frequencies need to be high as possible. This technique has been known for thousands of years. People from all sorts of different cultures have meditated to raise their personal power and reach states of enlightenment. There are numerous free wonderful meditation apps available, 'Insight Timer' is one very good one. If you have never given one a try I would definitely recommend that you do.

SUMMARY

- To gain the most in life successfully we need to keep our vibrations at the highest level as possible.
- Raise your vibration by eating the right foods.
- Food is also made up of energy. If we are to raise our own vibrational frequency, eating foods high in energy vibration is a great way to start.
- Eating high energy food will help us reach higher consciousness and we can better connect with our higher source.
- As well as eating food energised by the sun, spending time outdoors in the fresh air under the sun is a great way to raise energy.
- Other actions you can take in establishing the highest vibration are, exercising, drinking filtered water and having positive thoughts.
- Meditation is a great way to increase positive energy.

- The time taken in mediation brings about a freshness of the mind and revived energy.

CHAPTER EIGHT

THE SCIENCE BEHIND IT ALL

Now for those of you reading this, that prefer a more scientific understanding of the world we live in, I have included some information on a science that specializes at looking into, and studying consciousness and the power it may have. The Institute of Noetic Sciences (IONS) is an organisation that is carrying out scientific research into consciousness and its role in the physical world.

In Dan Brown's book 'The Lost Symbol,' Noetic Science is mentioned. Noetic research is published in many science journals but is still not widely known about. Noetic comes from an ancient Greek word meaning inner wisdom. Noetic Science is a multidisciplinary field that brings scientific research into subjective inner wisdom to try to study the full range of human experience. It focuses on the mind-body connections. There are several ways we can focus and understand the world we live in. Science uses observation, experiments, evaluating and measurements to get a deeper understanding, but there are other ways of knowing things about the world around us. These are our subjective, internal understandings. The gut feelings we get, hunches, intuitions.

The sort of experiences that cannot be explained or proven. This way of knowing is called Noetic.

I have a powerful story to share with you that will explain to some degree why I believe in the power of our senses and internal knowledge. This experience is still vividly clear in my mind. The tragic event occurred two weeks after my son, Benjamin was born. I had a dream this one night, that was as clear as can be. Not blurry or bizarre. In my dream I was stood in a cemetery standing over a lowered coffin in the ground. A voice asked me in my head, "would you be sad if Alan died?" Now Alan was my mother's husband. They had met after I had left home. I knew Alan, but our relationship was not as close as it would be if he had brought me up. In my dream I took a moment to answer the question as I looked around the grave. My mother was there, as well as Alan's grown up daughter and grown up son. I answered, "yes," I would be sad if Alan died because I knew the pain that the people who loved him would feel. That was when I woke up. The dream really bothered me. It bothered me enough to tell my husband about it.

Now Alan was seemingly fit and healthy. We had absolutely no idea that he was ill in anyway. We had not been discussing his health or had any concerns. He was only 49 years old, so Alan dying was not a thought on anybody's mind. Anyway, as you do, I shrugged the dream off and actually completely forgot about it. Later in the day the memory still did not come back, even after the shock of what occurred a few hours later.

A couple of hours later I was feeding my two-week old baby, and my mother was studying at her house which was only a couple of miles away from mine. Alan and mum had recently started jogging. This particular morning Alan went jogging alone so my mum could work on assignments for her degree. Now Alan would usually only be gone 15 minutes but he did not come back. Alan never returned. My mother started to realise he had been out a long time. She went out looking for him, rang his mobile, and ended up wondering whether she had made a mistake. Perhaps he had said he was going somewhere straight from his run, but when she checked, his car was still parked outside their flat. Eventually mum rang me to tell me she couldn't find Alan. I went over with Ben and we walked around the local town and the only thought that came into my mind was whether he had just up and left her. I did not remember my dream at all. We were completely confused. Eventually mum said she would ring the police. I agreed, that there really was nothing else she could do. I went back to my house to feed Ben and left her to it. Mum rang my home not long after I got back to say that she had rang the police and they were coming over. Now I was shocked at this, but mum felt it must just be normal procedure. I went and fed Ben and then another call came through. My husband picked the phone up, but knowing it would be my mum he just picked up the phone and started to hand it to me. As the phone was coming closer to my ear I could hear screaming and I realised my mum was shouting "he's dead!"

Alan had gone jogging that morning and two older ladies saw him fall to the ground. They went for help but Alan had died immediately from a heart attack. The post mortem showed that Alan had needed a quadruple bypass, none of us knew. Not even Alan. I went with my mother to identify Alan's body and got home to my family very late. Once in, my husband just quietly said, "Do you remember what you dreamt last night?" In all of the day's crazy events I had not remembered at all. I was stunned when I was reminded and also very glad that I had mentioned my dream before the day's tragedy. Mentioning after, that I had dreamt Alan died would may have been doubted by others and maybe by then even myself.

I have absolutely no doubt that we all hold inner knowledge and powers that we may not be completely aware of. With science investigations I am sure it won't be long before we are able to understand more. For some this knowledge is already there. Believe now that you are more powerful than you have ever realised and you can learn to develop your personal skills. I do not know why I dreamt of Alan's death the night before he died. Perhaps one day, science like Noetic science will be able to explain how this was possible. All I strongly feel, because of these sort of incidents, is that there is more to our abilities than perhaps we are aware of.

Noetic may be a word used for centuries, but the term Noetic Sciences was first used in 1973, when the Institute of Noetic Sciences (IONS) was founded by the astronaut Edgar Mitchell. On his return from the moon Mitchell recalls feeling a profound sense of universal connectedness. He later described this feeling as a 'Samadhi' experience: "The presence of divinity became almost palpable, and I knew that life in the universe was not just an accident based on random processes…The knowledge came to me directly."

It doesn't matter if you believe in a God or not, all that truly matters here is that you realise that you are not probably aware of your own mental and spiritual capabilities. I get so excited at this thought. You could be on the verge where you start to realise our own powers. Use these understandings to learn about yourself and to create the life you desire.

When I discuss creating the life you want and the power that you hold in your mind I am not suggesting for one second that thinking about Alan dying brought the act about. It was the other way. He was obviously dying and somehow I picked up on whatever energy was surrounding Alan. Although I did not consciously realise this, in my dream state my subconscious new it. Alan was not a well man even though it was not realised at the time. His energy must have known, that time was short for him. Somehow I picked up on it. Never underestimate your hunches or gut instincts. Start to learn to work with them. You are getting messages from a powerful source when you experience them. Too many people ignore these instincts, but they are instincts that we have been provided with. If you learn to work with them, decisions you make in life could be far better decisions than if you push those natural instincts out of the way and ignore them.

Animals have these instincts. They do not question them or ignore them. Dogs can sense, if someone is kind. We should take a leaf out of their book. Recently, there have been numerous reports in the press of dogs sensing when their owners are ill before it is realised by the owner themselves. Perhaps they can smell illness or perhaps they just sense it. At this moment in time we do no really know which it is. Learn to trust your instincts, work with them instead of ignoring them. The wisdom inside of you could be a very powerful source if you learn to use it well.

SUMMARY

- Noetic Science is a multidisciplinary field that brings scientific research into subjective inner wisdom to try to study the full range of human existence.
- The term Noetic Sciences was first used in 1973, when the institute of Noetic Sciences (IONS) was founded by the astronaut Edgar Mitchell.
- Never underestimate your hunches or gut instincts. Start to learn to work with them.
- The wisdom inside of you is very strong, you need to learn to trust it.

CHAPTER NINE

MINDSET

In this chapter, I want you take some time to consider mindsets in relation to how you view yourself and your life. Mindset plays a very important role when it comes to living a fulfilled and happy existence. When born, the human brain is remarkably unfinished in comparison to other animals. Some animals walk within hours of being born. They are born with pre-programmed brains. Humans, on the other hand, are completely dependent for a very long time on those around them. The reason for this is so that they can grow into the environment in which they were born. This makes humans far more flexible than other species. However, as we grow, some of us start to lose this flexibility due to the messages we receive from the people around us. Therefore, we become shaped by our personal experiences. We stop growing. But you are not an animal. You have the ability to always change and grow. Here's the thing – you just need to do it.

Undeniably, some of us have had a better start in life than others. But tough starts can give you a stronger resolve than those who have maybe had it easier. There are always lessons to learn from hardship. Many of the most successful people in this world have experienced some truly tough challenges to get where they are. I am sure that you have heard of many stories in your lifetime of people who have achieved great things despite major setbacks. These are the people who did not accept that their situation would hold them back. They knew in their heart that they could make a success for themselves and so, dear reader, can you.

Look at Stephen Hawking. There is absolutely no doubt that he is an exceptionally clever man. He achieved so much before being diagnosed with ALS, a form of Motor Neurone Disease shortly after his 21st birthday. Even though he is wheelchair dependant and has to rely on a computerised voice system to communicate, he is able to still carry out research and balance his family life alongside. A huge amount of his success has come since his diagnosis, he is just one person who has shown that our life's circumstances are not always strict boundaries. You can achieve great things. We will all have different obstacles but they can be worked with.

If we can achieve our dreams, then we may question why we are not all highly paid, successful, happy, super fit individuals? The reason could be down to the fact that although many of us would love all the trimmings in life, we may not do what is considered necessary to achieve them. We may also not believe that we are capable of achieving them. Our mindset could be working against us here. We need to realise our true capabilities as humans. As a baby and as a young child, we did not question our abilities. We will have been very curious. We learnt about ourselves and our capabilities continuously. Day by day pushing our boundaries soaking up new achievements. But for many of us, over time, we stopped pushing boundaries as we were taught about barriers and restrictions from the people around us. Many reaching a standstill with personal progression and growth. Perhaps due to lack of confidence or a disbelief that we could reach further goals. This lack of conviction in our personal abilities can be so restraining in our life's journey. Can you just imagine for one second where your life could lead if you had complete conviction in your abilities or at least a determination to try to go out there and attempt to grasp all that you desire. If you feel like there must be more to life than you are currently experiencing, then you are very likely to be correct.

One of the main contributing factors for the stunting of personal growth and development as adults is down to our desire to conform. As we grow we start to be aware of the behaviours of those around us. To feel comfortable, and to fit in, we begin mirroring this pattern of behaviour. You only have to take a look at a group of teenagers to see this in action. Most will be wearing similar clothes, have similar hairstyles and display similar behaviours. Even as we grow older without even consciously being aware of it people tend to carry on with this mirroring. The problem is that we tend to be mirroring the wrong people! Ask a group of school children what they wish for in their future, and the answer is very likely to be along the lines of being successful and happy in some way. At this point, they may be excited about their prospects. But unfortunately many will not succeed in their ambitions for their future. How is it that so many of us don't accomplish what we hankered for as a younger person? Why do so many of us end up in jobs that we don't like, or in relationships that are not quite right? Or doing things that is the opposite from what we wanted years back? I do not believe it is down to the fact that we are not capable, I believe we are all capable of amazing things but many of us inadvertently began to conform to the norm. We tend to be able to grasp the notion that if we do not stretch our body and move it regularly that over time we would lose flexibility. Could it also be possible that this occurs with our minds? If we do not keep stretching it with new ideas, knowledge and experiences we could start to become somewhat stagnant and then perhaps our behaviours become less flexible?

When we see the same pattern around us time and time again, it is easy to understand that we see that pattern as normal – the way it is. We have all seen people working long hours in jobs that they are not really satisfied with. They may make good money, or some may not, but for many people, working long hours is just the way they believe it is supposed to be. They are probably working those long tedious hours to attain the necessities in life, some luxuries and attempting to retire in some form of comfort. Sadly, for many, that doesn't occur even with the long hours.

Some people do not conform with what the majority are doing. For many of these people their lives are far more successful and fulfilled. Wouldn't you rather be one of them? These people sometimes manage to work less hours on careers they love. Loving what you are doing is vitally important when you consider how much of your life you will be working. Shouldn't our goal be to live our life rather than just survive it? Some people just seem to grasp that life does not have to be so difficult. There will always be ups and downs. As long as you accept when things go wrong and learn from it. Many of us struggle to shake off let downs and can use the bad experience as a reason to never try again. We can tend to play it a lot safer after a negative occurrence. Lessons can be learnt but don't let it stop you reaching for the stars. Life is for living and enjoying, not just persevering. To be successful in life, you need to feel fulfilled and achieved. Your idea of success may be bringing up a healthy happy family that brings you so much joy that you are fit to burst. It could mean helping others to achieve their greatness. Whatever it means to you, you have the means inside of yourself to achieve it. Find what makes you happy – find your passion and build a life around that, rather than fitting that passion in after you have spent most of the time working to survive. I know I may be simplifying it somewhat, we do all have bills to pay but we can tend to complicate things. The more money that we earn the more overheads we tend to accumulate. Simplifying our financial burdens could lead to a much happier existence. We all probably know of people who earn very well but who are also stressed because of the lavish lifestyle they have created. Wanting luxuries is not a bad thing but we need to consider the cost, financially as well as emotionally.

So, let us take a look at your mindset and see if this could play a factor in the shaping of your life and who you are today.

Your mindset could make all the difference to the life that you are leading.

Do you have a fixed mindset or a growth mindset?

Do you know?

To succeed in any area of life then you really need a growth mindset. If you don't have one, then fortunately with effort that can be changed, if you so choose. If your mindset is fixed, then even if you want success, you fear failure more. If this is the case for you, then consider what your life would look like without fear. I truly believe that if fear did not exist, more of us would be living the life we dreamed of. Fear holds so many of us back. Life is precious and relatively short, so make the most of it and sort your mindset out. To improve your life, you are going to need this growth mindset. By having this type of mindset, you will be happy to try and stretch yourself in all areas that you want to improve. Having this mindset doesn't guarantee that you will always be successful. Yes, you could still fail, but you will not resign yourself to beliefs of 'being a failure.' You will learn from that failure, and then with new lessons and knowledge on-board you will try again, but this time a little wiser. Everyone fails from time to time. The difference, however, and the very important factor, is how you look at that failure. If failure in the past crippled you with self-doubt and negative thoughts, then your mindset definitely needs to change. Day always follows night and success will follow failure, but only if you try again with the new knowledge learnt. It is not the winning or losing that you should be focusing on; consider the lessons you have learned from the whole experience. This applies to every area in your life. If something didn't work, try again but this time differently. Successful people are not people who have never failed – they are people who never gave up. Toughen up on the failing front and who knows where it will lead. If you tried a cruise holiday and found you hated being on the ship, that wouldn't put you off the idea of going on holiday forever, would it? No, you would just try something different next time. Learn from the experience, because until you try, you will never know.

Richard Bandler and John Grinder, the creators of neuro-linguistic programming (NLP), believe there is actually no such thing as failure. Imagine that – how wonderful our lives would be if failure had never been brought into it. NLP states that instead of failure we get feedback. In essence, everything we do is an achievement. What a great philosophy to live by, and how true! We always learn something from experiences. Even if we didn't achieve the exact desired results, we are still closer than we were before we tried. If you can take this mindset on board then life becomes an enjoyable learning experience.

Your true potential is completely unknown, and all you need to do is keep pushing to achieve as much as you can and see where it takes you. Do not put boundaries on yourself or allow others to restrain you. You are free to try and try and try. As soon as children get to an age where they can evaluate themselves, problems start to occur for many. Some become afraid to make mistakes, and so they give up on opportunities, out of fear of failure or looking silly. We start to label ourselves as people who aren't very good at this and that, and we say things such as 'I could never do that.' But why not? Who says so? You? A fixed mindset is created. If we had kept a positive growth mindset, a mind where we believed that anything was possible, then we would happily give things a try. To achieve your full potential, you need this growth mindset.

NASA rejected applications from applicants that had histories of just success. They chose applicants that had endured significant failures in their lives but had bounced back. They understood that a stronger character is formed when someone fails but doesn't give up. Do not be afraid of failing in any area of your life. The lessons learnt from that failure will help you succeed in the future. Failure at anything should not define you. It is merely an experience that you have had. Learn from it and move on. You didn't question your abilities as a very young child learning the hardest skills of all, in such a relatively short space of time. When you still couldn't walk after a certain amount of trying, you didn't say 'that's it, I'm never trying that again,' did you? There was no time limit on learning, so why do we put time limits on things as we get older? Anyone can become successful at any age. It doesn't matter how long it takes. What matters is that you get there and enjoy the journey along the way. I am sure you have heard the stories of the most successful people in their field being turned down time and time again, to then become amazingly successful because they didn't give up on their dreams. Don't give up on yours. That would be the failure. That would be the time you have actually failed. Ending up at the end of this amazing time on Earth and realising that you just didn't give yourself the chance. Take a look at a big large tree – trees become stronger the more they are blown about by wind. Trees that are protected from the wind never grow as strong. The same can go for people. The harder the knocks, the stronger we become.

You may accept that you probably do have a fixed mindset in some area of your life, but how can you change it? You can alter your mindset to a positive one firstly by listening to your self-talk. If you find that you are putting yourself down, then stop. These are the times when you hear yourself say 'I am so stupid,' 'I can never do that,' 'I will always be fat'. As soon as you hear these words, stop and change them. Positive affirmations are what your mind needs to hear. 'I can learn anything,' 'I can do that,' 'I am slim and healthy'. You may not be any of these things yet, but the first step is to believe. That is a very important step.

Whilst working on my own personal growth and development, I realised that for many years I definitely had a fixed mindset. I wanted to achieve things and be successful, but the fear of failing held me back massively. I did not realise that by not doing things in life I was failing immediately. I chose immediate failure over aiming towards success. Then, I could always comfort myself by believing that if I had tried, I would have succeeded. Do you want to spend the rest of your life thinking that you really could have done this and that if only you had tried? As I've worked on my growth I have become less afraid of failing. I am more interested in trying. I am now aware that if it doesn't work out, I will at least be satisfied in the knowledge that I will have learned a lot from the experience. I won't spend the rest of my years wondering 'what if.' This book is an example of that. I have wanted to write for years. Fear of doing a bad job however, stopped me from doing so. Now I feel proud of the fact I have given it a go. I have undoubtedly learned a lot from the process and thoroughly enjoyed writing it. Therefore, if it doesn't end up being successful, I can at least tell people that yes, I wrote a book. How fantastic will that be? I wrote a book! It may have been harder than I thought, but I am happy that I did it and that I gained valuable experiences along the way. There is always the possibility that this book will be a great book. Someone may even read it! Someone may even love it! They may learn from it and grow themselves. It may be exactly what someone needed to inspire them to go out there and enjoy life more. I will be very happy in the knowledge that I will have succeeded with my original desire. Only time will tell, but whatever the outcome, I will have achieved something.

Take a look at all areas of your life and ask yourself which mindset you have been facing them with. You may find that in some areas you use a growth mindset, and in others a fixed one. This can happen – we aren't always one or the other. For me I had a growth mindset when it came to my family life and relationships but it was my personal growth, such as my career and learning, that I was closed down on. You will find the areas with a fixed mindset are the areas that you would like to change and this can be done.

Don't be someone who is too shy to go out there and push themselves to learn what their own limits are. You have been designed to learn, grow and push boundaries. Life is far too short to be so self-conscious. So if this is you, then make sure you work on your growth mentality and create a character that is strong and confident. Once you have done that, you can go out there with your head held high and absolutely smash it!

Acknowledging the fact that you need to change will actually start the changing process immediately, as it is the 'not-understanding' that keeps you in the wrong place. Another way to help change your mindset is based on goals. Get a piece of paper and write down a list of all the things you would like to achieve if there were no restraints on you - no financial concerns, no time issues, no family issues. A long list crafted out of everything that you would love to achieve. On the list put short term goals, like the things you would like to get done tomorrow. These may be little things like ringing a friend or a small job you keep putting off. Break your list down into smaller goals and larger goals. Then out of these make a list for daily tasks, weekly tasks, monthly, yearly and so on. The reason you want to be writing down smaller tasks is because when you achieve them and tick them off, your sense of achievement grows and grows. Over time, you will start to feel that you are someone who can get things done. This new sense of self growth will grow as quickly as a snowball rolling down a hill. Self-confidence comes from achievements, but these achievements do not have to be large. A sense of achievement can come from deciding to have a family games night and actually doing it. Tick those goals off your list as you carry them out and see how it makes you feel. It feels fantastic. Going to bed at night knowing what you have achieved that day, that week, that month or that year is one wonderful feeling. Your achievements will keep on growing and new goals will keep on emerging.

I never used to get things finished. I was renowned for getting so excited about new things, starting them and then just not finishing them. When I finally saw something through to the end, the sense of achievement was massive. So massive in fact, that I actually burst into tears with pride. This feeling was amazing and addictive, and I wanted to feel it again. So don't forget, actually carrying out tasks and goals brings positivity into your life in many ways. Your self-worth and confidence both grow, and you begin to realise that you can get anything done that you decide to do. We can all make excuses for not finishing things but we should aim to be someone who does whatever it takes to accomplish a goal. Excuses leave you feeling a failure inside. Even if it doesn't matter to anybody else, it actually matters to you. How have you felt when you cancelled on an arrangement just because you really couldn't be bothered with it? The feeling that you're left with is a feeling that is really not worth having. The feeling that you would have experienced from going ahead with the plans, in contrast, is wonderful. It doesn't matter how big or small the achievements are – even small achievements build up a confidence internally. What you need to remember is that you are someone that can get the job done. Your mindset will accept this new version of you and will help you do what it takes to get things accomplished. So realise the importance of achievements. Set goals for yourself. Big and small. Do not be afraid to fail. Lessons will always be learnt and personal growth will follow.

SUMMARY

- Mindset plays a very important role when it comes to living a successfully fulfilled life.

- If you are not satisfied with you, you can do something about it - change.

- Find your passion and build a life around that.

- If your mindset is fixed, then even if you want success you fear failure more.

- It is not the winning or losing that you should be focusing on; it should be the lessons you learned from the whole experience.

- There is no such thing as failure, just feedback.

- A stronger character is formed when someone fails but doesn't give up.

CHAPTER TEN

USING YOUR MIND FOR INSTANT HAPPINESS

I would like us to now look at the actual process of thinking itself. What seems to be a simple natural act can have a profound effect on our stress levels and our overall happiness. Apparently we have around 50,000 to 70,000 thoughts per day. That's a lot of thinking. Now I am sure you have experienced the wonderful sensation when a constant background noise suddenly goes quiet. Sometimes you only notice how noisy it was, when it finally stops. Our internal chatter is something many of us do not give much consideration to. Becoming aware and sometimes having a break from this internal chatter can be extremely beneficial to our state of mind. To really become fully present in a moment, without missing any of it through distraction, can be such an uplifting experience. People can discuss wonderful times that they have had. Perhaps a family walk, but are they truly present? Maybe they were there but not completely focused in the moment. Even in times like family walks, when we could be benefitting hugely from the moment itself, we can find ourselves distracted by internal reflections. Reflections that have nothing to do with the present moment. If you are guilty of this and most of us are, working on mindfulness will ensure you fully start to immerse yourself into a worthy moment. The benefits you will receive can be amazing. When you meet up with someone you haven't seen for ages and spend time chatting away, catching up on everything, you can literally feel exhausted afterwards. For many of us, this is exactly what is going on in our head most of the time, unless we make the effort to cease it. It is beneficial to have times in the day when you just become absorbed in the present moment and only that moment. We tend to be focusing on so many things at once in life, leaving us permanently warn out. We are not always appreciating exactly what is occurring in our life at the present time. It is not as beneficial taking a walk in nature if we spend the time thinking about work. Become mindful of those special moments and those moments will become even more advantageous. It can be the very simple things in life that we could be appreciating more. For example, those extra few minutes in bed before we have to get up. Embrace those moments, become fully aware of them, instead of jumping forward in your mind to all the things you need to get done that day. Many of us are constantly exhausted and this thought process could have a lot to with it. Try to enjoy peaceful moments without allowing your mind to distract you. If you practice mindfulness you will find you have more energy to deal with the day to day jobs that need sorting without all the stress. Being in the now can have an amazing positive effect on your mental well-being.

Do you actually live in the present moment at all times? Or do you find yourself thinking about past situations or worrying about future ones? We all have a past. It is littered with good times and bad times. When we think back, for most of us, it is to think over the pain that we have endured. Doing this takes us back to that unhappy place which we then relive all over again, like a movie in our mind. The outcome of the problems we have experienced will always be same, we cannot change them by thinking over them again and again. So why do we continue to do it? It certainly isn't to make us feel better. We will always be left feeling the hurt felt at the time. Nothing changes there. It will only leave you sad. By repeatedly thinking on an issue you are giving it the power to hurt you over and over again. Seriously, wasn't once enough?

Make a decision to start to accept your past. You do not have to like it, just remember, it is over. The only way it can be kept alive is by replaying it. It is said that we can be our own worst enemy and when we live in the past this certainly is the case. Now you may spend time reminiscing the good things from your past. Reminiscing the happy times is great. Appreciating good times is wonderful. But if you're the sort of person who does this a lot, then it can sometimes be due to the believe that a past time was better than the present. This can cause us to be in a state of melancholy. Being happy about past situations is great, but what is more important, is that our present is great. The present is the only real time you have.

We all know of people who spend much of the time talking about their past. Do not be one of them! Next time you have a catch up with someone, be aware of your conversation and see if you tend to discuss past events and if so, stop! Surely you have present matters you can discuss. Do not be someone who blames their past, for their life situation now. Most of us have had some pretty awful experiences. Even with the worst sort of history, there are people out there that manage to grasp their present situations and live an amazing life. Let's be one of those people. You can only benefit from that. It can become habitual that we go round in circles making excuses for our unhappy state. Blaming this situation and that situation for our present state. All habits can be broken but only once we realise that we are doing it. Einstein defined insanity as doing the same thing over and over again and expecting different results. Stop doing it. If you find yourself going in circles you can actually stop. The way to put an end to it, is to do something different to your usual pattern. Habits can be broken.

When we talk about the past to make excuses for our present situation, we are playing the blame game. Blaming that situation for the place we are in now. We have all heard of amazing people who have gone through some horrendous experiences that achieve such great things. You can be one of them. Sound too difficult? It isn't you just have to choose to except and move on. You can do anything you believe you can. So if you are reading this and thinking thoughts along the line of, I can never change the life I have because of the life I have had, then sadly you'll be correct. I am hoping though that you are reading this and thinking, I can move on and start living the life that I desire starting right now.

Like most I've had my share of struggles and unhappiness. My mum brought three of us up by herself which was obviously a financial struggle for her. As a young teenager I suffered with anorexia then bulimia. As an adult I've struggled in the past with depression and anxiety issues. Instead of now having these past issues hold me back I only consider them as a lesson to learn from, so that I hopefully will never experience these issues again. We all know that great things can come from hard situations so make your life's problems be the kick up the bum you need to go out there and change your life for the better. Other people manage it, so be one of them and be proud of who you become.

The happiest people seem to be the ones that see freshly with new eyes every day. These people tend to look at life in a childlike manner. They don't let past events taint their experiences. Try not be someone who is stuck in the past. It can ruin years and years of your life and sadly for some, it can ruin their whole life. Life goes by so quickly, so there is no time to waste literally wasting it. If you can wake up every morning appreciating that it is a brand new day you are more likely to enjoy the day ahead. As painful as our past can be, it is now only a memory. It is not what is happening in your life right now. For many people, they are sad because they constantly think about their past or they are anxious because they worry about their future. Worst, they go from worrying about the past to worrying about the future in an endless circle. Missing out on the experiences of the present moment. Thinking about times gone-by or times to come can mean that we miss the only real time in our lives, and that is right now. By keeping our mind right here where you are now you could instantaneously be happy and stay happy.

For those who think constantly in their future, maybe it's sometimes to worry about 'what ifs'. There is absolutely no point in wasting your precious time worrying about things that could happen. Half the time your concerns do not even occur so you have caused yourself worry over absolutely nothing at all. Worries are connected to our imagination and are not always connected to what is actually happening. It is a complete waste of your time worrying about what ifs. Amazingly we all get through situations. We all survive. Learn to be confident that you can survive anything. Enjoy the moment and live each day with fresh eyes. It is said that most of the things we worry about never actually occur so let's stop doing it. When you now find yourself running through scenarios in your head, stop and start living in the now. Here is an example of how my thoughts could change my mood completely right this minute. At this moment in time, I am writing down ideas for my book, something I am extremely happy about. I am not thinking about finishing it or if I can publish it, or even if anyone will buy it. I am enjoying the moment of actually just writing it. I am in the present. It's early morning and I am still under my cosy duvet as it's my favourite place to write. I have recently changed my bedding so I can smell the fresh sheets. The sun is coming through the windows. It's very early autumn here in Wales so getting a bit chillier first thing in the day. It is feeling lovely and fresh. I can hear birds outside singing obviously very happy to be alive. My little westie, Poppy, is curled up next to me. She is great company as I write. Next to me I have a hot cup of coffee, another one of my favourite things. So this is my absolute now, my only reality and it is all great.

Okay so like I mentioned, I could be thinking about the future and then my feelings could be very different. Not this content place I am in at the moment. I'd still be doing exactly the same thing, here writing in my bed but I'd be missing all the perfect moments that are actually occurring because I would be projecting into a 'maybe' future. If I start wondering if I am any good, I may start feeling that I am just wasting my time here, how am I possibly going to publish this? What if no one reads it? What if they do actually read it, and think it's a load of nonsense? How embarrassing is that going to be! I should stop writing now! Or I could be thinking in the past. Well, I've never done anything like this before. I have failed at so many things in my life, is this going to be just another thing I've failed at? I'm probably just wasting my time on a pipedream.

Can you see how thinking in the past or the future can bring a beautiful moment into an anxious one or a fearful one? Thinking in this manner is the reason why so many people give up on their dreams. If this is you then stop. Every time you find yourself projecting into the future or reminiscing into the past, stop and just take in exactly what is going on right at that moment. It is the only thing that is actually real in your life, the present.

SUMMARY

- By repeatedly thinking on an issue you are giving it the power to hurt you over and over again.

- The present is the only real time you have.

- Do not be someone who blames their past on their life situation now.

- Worries are connected to our imagination and are not always connected to what is actually happening.

- Enjoy the moment and live each day with fresh eyes.

- Every time you find yourself projecting into the future or reminiscing into the past, stop and just take in exactly what is going on right at that moment. It is the only thing that is actually real in your life, the present.

CONCLUSION

This book has been written with the sole intention to be a guide towards reaching a more fulfilled and happy life. We all need reminders from time to time on how to make the best of what we have been given. I hope that you truly believe in the power of yourself and understand that the life you want to lead and the person you want to be is all within your grasp. Creating a world for yourself and your loved ones that is perfect, still leaves the bigger question about the state of the world we live in today. Many of us are frightened by the huge problems we see occurring around us and many are wondering what this world is going to look like for the children of the future. The world's problems may not be sortable by the hands of one person, or even their positive thoughts but together we can make a difference. I strongly believe that we are at a point where change will happen because as a whole we can make that difference.

Since the 1990's Princeton University has been carrying out research on a global consciousness project. Their aim has been to see whether human consciousness can synchronize and act coherently together. They have been tracking the effects of events on a network of computers placed all around the world. These computers just churn out random numbers. In the Journal of Scientific Exploration in 2002, it was reported that when the attacks on the World Trade Centre occurred on

September 11th, 2001 a measurable effect on the random numbers also occurred. It is believed that the outpouring of emotion by so many people all over the world collectively altered the operation of the computers. There have been numerous times when this has occurred and it has always been put down to the collective thoughts of people all over the world. On the day of the trade centre attacks the world hurt. The world prayed. The world showed their love. This reaction seems to have changed the affects of the random computer system. Our thoughts as we have already seen can change reality for ourselves. Imagine what positive thoughts from people everywhere could bring about, for the world around us. If we all start thinking lovingly, we could start to see a domino affect. We can easily see how a kind word or a big smile affects one person. That person may take that lovely compliment and it could change their day positively. Their happy mood could affect people close by them. Let's start with ourselves and see how far feeling good can stretch.

I would like to share 'The Story of the Birthday of the World' told by Rachel Naomi Remen, M.D. Rachel's Orthodox Rabbi grandfather told her this story as her 4th birthday present:

'In the beginning there was only the holy darkness, the Ein Sof, the source of life. In the course of history, at a moment in time, this world, the world of a thousand thousand things, emerged from the heart of the holy darkness as a great ray of light.

And then, perhaps because this is a Jewish story, there was an accident, and the vessels containing the light of the world, the wholeness of the world, broke. And the wholeness of the world, the light of the world, was scattered into a thousand thousand fragments of light. And they fell into all events and all people, where they remain deeply hidden until this very day.

Now, according to my grandfather, the whole human race is a response to this accident. We are here because we are born with the capacity to find the hidden light in all events and all people, to lift it up and make it visible once again and thereby to restore the innate wholeness of the world. It's a very important story for our times. This task is called *tikkun olam* in Hebrew. It means the restoration of the whole world. And this is, of course, a collective task. It involves all people who have ever been born, all people presently alive, all people yet to be born. We are all healers of the world. This story opens a sense of possibility. It's not about healing the world by making a huge difference. It's about healing the world that touches you. That's around you. That's where our power is. Many people feel powerless in today's situation.'

So perhaps we are not as powerless as we may of thought. Perhaps residing in us all is everything that is needed to be the best we can be and at the same time exactly what the world needs.

I mentioned at the very beginning that the 'secret' to life has been known for centuries. But for many years' people tried to protect this understanding. The understanding that we all possess a power to achieve anything. Some kept the secret for selfish reasons. They wanted to achieve amazing lives but did not want others to attain the same. Others though, protected this knowledge out of fear. These people realised that if we could, in essence, think things into reality perhaps people may use this power for negative effect. Perhaps some will actually focus and spend their time working on causing others harm. I believe that this is just as possible as thinking great things into existence. Many people will be doing this unintentionally. You may realise now that you are one of them. Thinking how much you hate someone, wishing them bad luck or even harm will send out negative energies. When we talk about karma, perhaps what we are really seeing is the negative thoughts of others, taking affect. No matter how much you may wish someone harm, negative desires aimed towards someone else will actually come back and hurt you and your life in some way in the future. Pagans believed wishing harm to someone would bring back misfortune 'three-fold'. Whatever energy positive or negative you put out into the world will be returned to you, times three. If you have been hurt by someone the best way you can get revenge, so to speak, is by never intentionally giving that person another thought again. Completely letting go. Don't fall into the trap of wishing harm. This is a trap. Yes, you may see someone getting their comeuppance but you will inevitably be hurt in the process. A vicious circle will ensue. Get your own back by rising above it and living your life without negativity. Surely the best revenge is by showing others how happy and successful you are.

Now as we come to the end of the book, I hope you are feeling inspired and believe in yourself. Hell was described at the very beginning of this book as the moment just before death when you meet the other 'you'. The you that achieved all the things your heart desired. If you follow your dreams and spend time working on the life you truly desire, perhaps that moment when you meet the other 'you' will feel like heaven. The moment when you see the best version of yourself and recognise it as the person you became. Realising at this moment that you did it.

I have loved writing this book and I picture somebody…you, reading it and taking something positive away from it. I would love to hear from you. You can find me on Facebook and Instagram. If you would like to keep up to date with any new works I will be writing in the future my email is alexgeesonauthor@yahoo.com. Let me know about your personal journey and how your own life has been affected by the power in you.

WWW.ALEXGEESON.COM

Wishing you the happiest most successful future.

Alexandria

www.ingramcontent.com/pod-product-compliance
Ingram Content Group UK Ltd.
Pitfield, Milton Keynes, MK11 3LW, UK
UKHW020241250726
13967UKWH00001B/497

9 780995 745100